THE *COSTUMA D'AGEN*

PUBLICATIONS DE L'ASSOCIATION INTERNATIONALE D'ÉTUDES OCCITANES

V

Directeur de Collection

Walter Meliga

THE *COSTUMA D'AGEN*

A THIRTEENTH-CENTURY CUSTOMARY COMPILATION IN OLD OCCITAN TRANSCRIBED FROM THE *LIVRE JURATOIRE*

TRANSLATED AND WITH NOTES AND AN INTRODUCTION BY

F.R.P. AKEHURST

BREPOLS

Cover illustration: Bibliothèque municipale d'Agen MS 42 f. 40v (detail). Used by kind permission of the Bibliothèque municipale d'Agen.

ISBN 978-2-503-51920-3

D/2010/0095/20

Printed on acid-free paper

For my wife, Judith Marion Akehurst

TABLE OF CONTENTS

Preface

Art historian Professor Alison Stones proposed to me in 1999 that we should go to Agen together to examine an Old Occitan customary text, to which her attention had been drawn by the many illustrations it contained. Accordingly we went to the Archives départementales de Lot-et-Garonne, where thanks to the great kindness of the library staff, we were able to make a complete photographic record of the manuscript, on slides. These slides were then scanned into the computer, and it was from these electronic images that I set about transcribing the text. We subsequently rephotographed the text, using a digital camera, with somewhat better results.

There are at least four other manuscripts of the text, and three of these have already been edited and published. None of these other manuscripts was illustrated, however, and the most recently published version was from 1911. When I obtained perhaps the only copy of this edition in the United States (a doctoral thesis from Bordeaux), I found the pages uncut. I thought the text should be better known, and indeed the pictures should be made available to the general public.

The present edition includes a transcription of the *Costuma d'Agen*, a thirteenth-century law code from Agen, a town on the Garonne river, not far from its confluence with the river Lot. The manuscript used, Agen, Archives départementales de Lot-et-Garonne MS 42, was an official copy, on which persons swearing an oath laid their hand. Hence it was referred to as the *Livre juratoire*. The text of the *Costuma d'Agen* in this manuscript is given in full, along with a facing page translation into English. The front and end material in the manuscript has not been translated. Since two of the other manuscripts contain five chapters not found in the *Livre juratoire*, I have included a transcription of them from a manuscript found in Stockholm, and an English translation (Appendix A). In addition, a number of charters from Agen are of interest, because they contain material very much like that of the *Costuma d'Agen*, or because they mention it, thus giving a terminus ad quem for its composition, although it may have existed in some form much earlier. I have provided the Old Occitan text of a few of these charters (Appendix B).

Professor Stones has kindly permitted me to reprint a shortened version of her description of the manuscript (Appendix C).

I have many persons to thank for their help and patience in the making of this book. First, of course, is Alison Stones, who first brought the manuscript to my attention, and with whom I had many discussions about it, some of them on the road from Périgueux to Agen. I wish to thank also Alfred Soman, late of the C.N.R.S., who helped with the photographing of the text. I must thank the International Travel Fund Committee of the College of Liberal Arts at the University of Minnesota for partial funding for one of my trips to Agen. I thank the Directrice des services d'archives de Lot-et-Garonne, Madame Martine Salmon-Dalas, for permission to see and photograph the manuscript, and then to publish the text. I thank Arvid Jakobsson and the Royal Library of Sweden, for help in obtaining a microfilm of the Stockholm manuscript, and for permission to publish extracts from it. I thank Peter T. Ricketts for discussions, advice, and encouragement, and Patrick Sauzet and Walter Meliga for suggestions for improvement. I thank various colleagues at the university of Minnesota for their en–couragement, including Kathryn L. Ryerson, Susan Noakes, and Stephanie Cain VanD'Elden, and Suzanne Garfield for help with formatting. Most of all I thank my wife, Judith M. Akehurst for her patience, especially during my annual visits to the manuscript and during the work of preparing this book. If any errors or omissions remain in this book, the responsibility is mine alone.

INTRODUCTION

Because northern France is thought of as the land of customary law, and southern France as the land of written (i.e. Roman) law, it may be surprising to some to learn that many southern French cities had their own customary laws written down in the thirteenth century in compilations called customaries. These customaries show a remarkable similarity to the northern French equivalents of the same period, with of course regional variations.

This book contains the Old Occitan text of the *Costuma d'Agen*, a compilation of the customary laws of the city of Agen, in southwestern France. An English translation on facing pages is provided. This is the first printed publication of the version of the *Costuma* that appears in a manuscript kept in the Archives départementales of the Lot-et-Garonne department, in Agen.[1] This manuscript was used as a "swearing copy" so called because people swearing oaths placed their hand on it. This manuscript will hereinafter be referred to as the *Livre juratoire,* whereas the other manuscripts will be referred to by distinguishing sigla, A, B, N, P, and S (see below). The manuscript published here, the *Livre juratoire*, is the ceremonial city copy of the *Costuma*, and is the only illustrated one.[2]

Manuscripts and editions

Three of the other manuscripts of the *Costuma d'Agen* have been previously published.[3] Because this Introduction will discuss the manuscripts and the editions, the extant manuscripts are listed here. For convenience, I adopt here the sigla used by all editors.

1. A. A *vidimé* on a parchment *rouleau* used by Moullié to make his edition. This manuscript is now in the Archives départementales de Lot-et-Garonne in Agen. The staff at the Archives were unable to trace this manuscript.

2. B. Bordeaux MS. Used by Barckhausen for his edition. Barckhausen refers to the manuscript simply as the *Livre des coutumes*, without giving a shelf number. When Barckhausen gives variants from A and P, it is apparent that B and P often agree against A. He evidently does not rely solely on the variants provided by Moullié.

---

[1] Agen, Archives départementales de Lot-et-Garonne, MS 42. The manuscript may be viewed on the WWW at the Archives départementales de Lot-et-Garonne website, in 2008 at http://www.cg47.fr/archives/coups-de-coeur/Tresors/tresors-archives.htm.

[2] The Noubel manuscript (Tropamer) (see note 3) has a couple of illustrated initials, no more, and no other illustrations. Many of the initials are pen-flourished. The Stockholm manuscript has one illustration in a lower margin, and another on an unnumbered folio at the beginning of the manuscript. These are not part of the original campaign.

[3] The three previously published editions are:

1. "Coutumes privilèges et franchises de la ville d'Agen," ed. Amédée Moullié, in *Recueil des Travaux de la Societe d'Agriculture, Sciences, et Arts d'Agen*, vol. 5 (Agen: Noubel, 1850), pp. 235-343. (Obtainable through http://gallica.bnf.fr). MS A

2. *Coutumes d'Agen* ed. Henri Barckhausen, in *Livre des coutumes de Bordeaux*, vol. 5, Archives municipales de Bordeaux (Bordeaux: Gounouilhou, 1890), pp. 216-269. MS B

3. *La coutume d'Agen*, ed. and trans. Henry Tropamer, Thèse pour le doctorat (Bordeaux: Cadoret, 1911). MS N

3. N. Used by Tropamer for his edition. This manuscript was presented to the city of Agen by its purchaser, Henri Noubel, a former mayor of Agen. The manuscript is found today in Agen: Agen, Archives départementales de Lot-et-Garonne, MS 5.

4. P. Paris ms., known to Moullié only via a copy made by an unknown student at the Ecole des Chartes, but which nevertheless allows Moullié to give some variants in his edition. Moullié identifies the manuscript as Paris, Bibliothèque Nationale, section des manuscrits, carton CC (sic). This manuscript has never been edited as such. Barckhausen supplies variants from P that are not in Moullié's edition of A, but does not mention having used it for his edition. The staff at the Salle des manuscrits at the Bibliothèque nationale were unable to trace this manuscript.

5. S. Stockholm, Royal Library, B697, of which an edition was planned in the late 19th century, first by Professor V. Edv. Lidfors of the University of Lund, and then by H. Emile Rébouis, but it never appeared.[4] This manuscript may have been written around 1300.[5] It has a few illustrations in margins, but they are not part of the original conception.

6. V. Vatican MS. This appears to be the same as S (see above).[6]

7. J. The *Livre juratoire*, or swearing copy, used for the present edition. Agen, Archives départementales de Lot-et-Garonne, 42. I propose that this manuscript be given the siglum J. Moullié thought that this was the manuscript from which the others were copied.[7] But Moullié did not know about the Noubel or the Stockholm manuscripts, which contain five chapters not seen in the Agen *rouleau* nor in the *Livre juratoire.*

The filiation of the mss. is hard to establish. It is clear that *N* and the *Livre juratoire* are closely connected: each contains the same fragments from the gospels and a table of contents listing chapters from 1 to 38, although the *Livre juratoire* table lists also chapters 39-42, in another hand. The two manuscripts contain the same chapters, except that before the last three chapters *N* adds five chapters evidently not in the manuscript that was copied into A in 1369. The only trace of the "missing" chapter 42 is in the Table of Contents of the *Livre juratoire*.[8] Lauzun declares, without proof, that the *Livre Juratoire* is considered as "la copie la plus ancienne et c'est lui qui, depuis, a servi de modèle à tous les autres exemplaires."[9] B is a copy of part of the *Costuma d'Agen*, kept in a register in Bordeaux with other customary compilations from other cities, notably Bordeaux, and probably made at the end of the fourteenth century, or more precisely the second part of the reign of Richard II.[10]

---

[4] See Clémens, Jacques. "L'espace coutumier d'Agen au Moyen Age." *Revue de l'Agenais* (1982), pp. 3-19. Clémens is mostly concerned in this article with the area where the Agen customs were applied, but he gives more information about the contents of the Stockholm manuscript than appears elsewhere.

[5] Opinion of M. Alison Stones. Personal communication.

[6] The manuscript was never delivered to the Vatican library. The Vatican library expected it to be transferred from Stockholm, but it is still there. See Jacques Clémens, "L'espace coutumier d'Agen au Moyen Age."

[7] Amédée Moullié, "Notice sur les divers exemplaires manuscrits des Coutumes de la ville d'Agen," *Recueil des travaux de la Société d'agriculture, sciences et arts d'Agen*, 6 (1853), 154-180, at p. 163.

[8] A later hand has added chapters 39-42 to the original 38 in the table of contents of S. The chapters themselves are not in S.

[9] Lauzun, Philippe, "Le livre juratoire des consuls d'Agen," *Revue de l'Agenais*, 37 (1910), 385-394 at 385-386.

[10] Barckhausen, vol. 5, p. III.

First redaction[11] of the *Costuma d'Agen*

All commentators agree that some time in the thirteenth century, the laws of the city of Agen in southwestern France were written down in a systematic way in the local language, Old Occitan (Old Provençal). Appendix A contains a transcription of a document dated 1298 that clearly mentions the *written* customs for the first time. Another document, also excerpted in Appendix A, of 1302 also mentions the "book of customs." and transcribes three chapters that are in the manuscripts of the *Costuma d'Agen,* including the *Livre juratoire.* The official nature of this written law code was recognized in 1369 by Louis d'Anjou and the king.[12] The Latin documents confirming this recognition have been copied into the *Livre juratoire,* starting on the last vellum page of the customary proper (f. 93v) and continuing on two paper folios. The watermark on the paper indicates that it was manufactured by Ballande cadet, who was active in the eighteenth century. The texts present some difficulties, but they have been included in the present transcription. An illustrated official copy of the customs, kept in Agen, was prepared and now bears the shelfmark MS 42, the *Livre juratoire.* This manuscript contains some excerpts from each of the gospels.[13] The swearing pages contain an image of the Trinity, facing an image of the Virgin and Child.[14] These two pages are so smudged, dirtied, and mended that parts of them can hardly be made out today.

In several of the illustrations the book itself is depicted with someone swearing with his hand on the open book (ff. 17v, 40v, 46r., 56v and 81r.). Notations on a page bound with the *Costuma* manuscript record that it was rebound in 1633, and that it was again rebound in 1772.[15] These notations suggest that the book still served some public purpose right down to the time of the Revolution. Its pages contain in their margins hand written notes in Renaissance and later scripts. The names of the *jurats* for 1633 and of the members of the city council as elected from year to year are inscribed in folios at the back of the book for the years 1629 through 1708. Thus the manuscript as it exists today contains useful material quite apart from the text of the *Costuma* itself, which makes up the major part of the volume.

The date of the *Costuma d'Agen* and of the *Livre juratoire*

In determining the date of the *Costuma d'Agen,* it is important to distinguish between the existence of customs, the existence of a written text of the customs, and the existence of the *Livre juratoire.*

Various writers seem to have assumed that if there is a mention of the customs of some locality, they must have existed there in written form. This is the assumption that allows some scholars to date the first written form of the *Costuma d'Agen* to 1205 or

---

[11] I use the word "redaction" in the normal French sense of "writing down" and not in the sense more normal in American legal usage of "edited, with portions obliterated."

[12] Moullié, Amédée. "Notice sur les divers exemplaires manuscrits des coutumes de la ville d'Agen." *Recueil des travaux de la Société d'agriculture, sciences et arts d'Agen.* 6 (1853), pp. 154-180, at p. 158. At the time, a certified copy, or *vidimé*, was made. Moullié used this *vidimé* as a base for his edition in 1850. The *Livre juratoire* was at that time not available, although its existence was known.

[13] The same excerpts are found in N.

[14] *Livre juratoire* Ff. 7v and 8r.

[15] F. Br.

before. Does the confirmation of customs by the lord imply that there is a written version? If so, our documents might point to the existence of a redacted form in 1221 or 1248. Another assumption is that a charter containing words identical with portions of the *Costuma d'Agen* must be of an earlier date than the *Costuma* itself. Since such words appear in the Charter of 1221, it is assumed that the *Costuma* must have been written down after that date.

In 1205, the town of La Sauvetat-de-Savères was given a set of customs with the following words: "Damus et concedimus et confirmamus in villa Salvitatis de Saveriis illas consuetudines, quae in civitate Agenii esse noscuntur . . . "[16] and Paul Ourliac has deduced from this that the customs of Agen, were written down at that time. " On sait en effet que la coutume d'Agen a été rédigée dès 1205 puisqu'elle a été accordée à cette date aux habitants de La Sauvetat-de-Savères; il ne reste cependant aucun texte de cette ancienne rédaction, qui fut confirmée, augmentée et remaniée en 1370."[17]

Various other scholars have suggested dates for the first written text of the *Coutume d'Agen*. Since the manuscript used by the first editor of the *Coutume d'Agen*, Amédée Moullié, is dated 1369, several writers have assumed that this is the earliest manuscript. For example: "Le premier texte complet des Coutumes d'Agen est de février 1369."[18] Moullié himself opts for the first half of the thirteenth century: "...à l'époque de la rédaction des coutumes, c'est-à-dire, durant la premiere moitié du XIII siècle..."[19] However, Moullié is more circumspect as to the date of the *Livre Juratoire*:

> Il parut ... plus convenable pour une ville riche et puissante, d'avoir un exemplaire spécial destiné à figurer dans cette cérémonie. [i.e. the oath given by the new lord entering Agen for the first time.] En conséquence les consuls, *à une date qu'il est impossible de préciser*, en firent faire un, qu'on suppose avoir dû être orné de tout le luxe que comportait alors l'art des copistes.
>
> Cet exemplaire devint ce qu'on appela le *Livre Juratoire*." (my emphasis)[20]

Moullié's statement is, however, only conjecture, and Tropamer places the compilation of the *Livre juratoire* in the last quarter of the thirteenth century, basing his comment on palaeographic evidence and the appearance of the figures in the illustrations:

> La rédaction de ce *Livre juratoire*, comme du manuscrit Noubel, a dû être faite en deux fois. A quelle époque? Les trois derniers chapitres mis à part, il semble bien que ce soit dans le dernier quart du XIIIe siècle. Les vignettes nous montrent des contemporains de saint Louis et d'Alphonse de Poitiers, et l'écriture est bien celle de cette époque. En tous cas cette rédaction est postérieure à 1221. Le chapitre 5 *in fine*, les chapitres 28 et 61 sont la copie de deux chartes accordées par Raymond VII, comte de Toulouse, aux Agenais, les 21 et 22 août, 1221.[21]

---

[16] J. R. Marboutin, "Notice historique sur La-Sauvetat-de-Savères," Revue de l'Agenais, 28 (1901), pp. 158-178, at p. 164.

[17] Ourliac and Gilles (see below p. XXV), vol 2, p. 78

[18] Jules Andrieu. *Histoire de l'Agenais* (Marseille: Lafitte reprints, 1976). [Paris: Picard, 1893], p. 90.

[19] Moullié, "Notice," p. 165.

[20] Moullié, "Notice," p. 168.

[21] Tropamer, op. cit., p. 9. Tropamer is referring to chapter numbers in his edition of MS N. The two charters are actually both dated 25 August. Adolphe Magen and G. Tholin. *Archives municipales d'Agen. Chartes. Première série (1189-1328)* (Villeneuve-sur-Lot, 1876), Charters X, XI, pp. 12-14.

Another piece of evidence is the *Coutume de Montpezat*, much of which is very similar to the *Costuma d'Agen*. A fourteenth-century French translation provides the date of the giving of these customs as 1279 and states they were written down by an Agen notary, Hélie Calvary. It seems unlikely that Calvary wrote down customs for the little town of Montpezat when there was no written version of the customs they copied.[22] It can be conjectured, therefore, that a written copy of the *Costuma d'Agen* existed in 1279, whether or not it has survived. Ten years later the customs of Agen were again awarded to other towns, this time south of the Garonne.[23]

The first mention in the published charters of a book containing the *Costuma d'Agen* is from 1298. This charter is reproduced in Appendix A. There are, however, many earlier and later mentions in the charters of the customs themselves, rather than of a book containing them, and some of the charters include language more or less identical to that found in certain provisions of the customs. For example, already in 1196/97, one hundred and fifteen citizens are listed as witnesses or cosignatories to a charter that begins: "Conoguda causa sia a totz omes qui son e serau que.l cossels d'Agen e li proome so acordat cum mantengo los dregs e las costumas de la vila a bona fe e ses enguan, e deu ne estre creutz lo cossels que o autreje sober lor sagrament, ..."[24] The very words that begin this document contain the rule that will be maintained in the *Costuma d'Agen* itself, and in other charters stretching into the fourteenth century,[25] namely that the customary law of Agen is what the city council declares it to be. The same rule appears in the charter of 1221, given by the future Raymond VII of Toulouse, who says "autrejam e cofermam totas lors costumas aissi quo melhs las an agudas e tengudas ilh ni li lor ancessor...*e si, sobre las costumas de la ciutad d'Agen se movia contrast entre nos e ·ls ciutadas o entre los ciutadas e nostre badles, nos ne creirem los .XII. proshomes del coselh; e si coselh no avia en la vila, nos ne creirem los .XII. proshomes de la meissa vila, que sian de bona renomnada, sobre lor sagramen que aisso que ilh autrejaran que sia costuma que nos o crezem e autrejam e cofermam als sobredits ciutadas per nos e per los nostres en durabletad...*"[26] (my emphasis) This whole charter with its method of proving customs by the council, is repeated in 1306 in Charter CXXXIV, when it seems certain that the customs had already been written down (see above).

In 1248, the whole citizenry seems to have been involved in drawing up municipal statutes, which largely govern behavior, as a result of unspecified civic problems. One of the provisions is that no citizen is to be blamed for a vigorous defense of the city's customs: "Derrecaps, que negus no serque ni fassa, per si ni per autrui, mal ni dapnatge a negu home d'Agen, per negu genh, ni en neguna manera, per mantener e per defendre las costumas e las franquessas de la vila d'Agen e.ls establiments del meiss loc..."[27] These provisions, however, do not repeat the provisions of the *Costuma d'Agen*, but

[22] Calvary included, no doubt on the orders of the local lord, several local provisions concerning markets, and omitted several chapters of the *Costuma d'Agen*, notably those concerning the salt monopoly, and the fees for notaries, which would have been inapplicable in Montpezat.
[23] Charters LXXXI, 1289, and LXXXIII, 1290, Magen and Tholin, pp. 133, 136.
[24] Charter II, Magen and Tholin, p. 2.
[25] For example Charter CXVI: "..dictus syndicus...obtulit se paratum docere et fidem facere de predicta consuetudine et usu per predictos consules vel per duodecim alios probos viros Agenni ..." Magen and Tholin, p. 196.
[26] Charter XI, Magen and Tholin, p. 14
[27] Charter XLIV, Magen and Tholin, p. 61.

supplement them. One might therefore conjecture that the written customs already existed at that time and were for that reason not repeated in Charter XLIV.

Did the written customs exist already in 1248? Poumarède asserts: "La rédaction definitive des coutumes contenues dans le *Livre Juratoire* doit se situer entre 1250 et 1270, comme l'attestent l'étude paléographique du manuscrit et l'examen des dessins à la plume accompagnant le texte, qui paraissent représenter des personnages de l'époque de Saint Louis."[28] Here, Poumarède appears to be relying on the word of Tropamer, but pushing Tropamer's dates back by a quarter century.[29]

An argument for an early date for a written version of the *Costuma d'Agen* would be the mention of the customs sworn to by citizens of Agen in 1196, just after the lordship passed from Richard I of England to Raymond of Toulouse as a dowry for Richard's sister. A prudent city council might well have written down the customs at that time, in order to ensure continuity when the lordship passed to Toulouse. Another argument would be that Richard granted their customs to the citizens of Marmande in 1182 and the written text of the early part of the Marmande customary seems to go back to that time.[30] Marmande is only a few miles from Agen, and it is plausible that Richard could have granted their customs to the Agen citizens on or about the same date as the Marmande concession, thus allowing the citizens to refer to them in 1196/7. But there is no record of this. Indeed the various manuscripts are all undated except A.

An argument for a later date is that Philippe IV the Fair confirms the customs in 1295, copying into this confirmation the words of the 1248 confirmation by Raymond VII, but without stating that the customs exist in written form.[31] Another argument for a later date is that the method of proving a custom in Agen remains the sworn testimony of the Consuls, or twelve good men, as seen in a charter from 1299.[32] There is no mention of proving a custom by reference to a *written* text until 1311.[33]

The *Livre juratoire* is claimed by some scholars to be the manuscript from which the others were copied. For this to be so, the absence of the five "new chapters" from this manuscript must be explained. Two of the manuscripts, namely the *rouleau* containing the *vidimé* of 1370, supposedly still in Agen, and the missing Paris manuscript, must be found and examined. There is obviously still some work to be done here, and a stemma to be drawn. The latter is beyond the scope of the present inquiry. Moullié imagines a scenario where the citizens of Agen have a specially copied and illustrated manuscript compiled, at a date which he declares impossible to determine, and that this manuscript is the *Livre juratoire*. This is plausible, but so self-evident as to be not helpful.

Some light can be shed on the writing of the *Livre juratoire* by an examination of its scribes and illustrations. A more detailed account of the codicology of the *Livre juratoire*

---

[28] Jacques Poumarede, *Géographie coutumière et mutations sociales. Les Successions dans le sud-ouest de la France au moyen âge* (Paris: Presses universitaires de France, 1972), p. 96.

[29] Tropamer, p. 9.

[30] Ourliac and Gilles, vol. 1, p. 102.

[31] Charter XCVI, Magen and Tholin, p. 163, confirming XLVI, p. 67.

[32] Charter CXVI Magen and Tholin, p. 194.

[33] Charter CXLI: "…Geraldus de Tastis..baronibus et consulibus villarum et locorum Agenni, *lecta sibi ibidem presentialiter consuetudine Agenni scripta in libro consulum Agennesii*, … juravit…quod ipse erit eisdem bonus dominus et legalis, secundum tenorem et continentiam consuetudinis predicte, prout continetur *in dicta consuetudine lecta ibidem*, …" (my emphasis) Magen and Tholin, p. 271.

has been provided by the kindness of M. Alison Stones, and appears as Appendix C. A fuller account will appear in Professor Stones' book on the illustrated medieval manuscripts of south western France (forthcoming).

The composition of the *Livre juratoire*

A. Chapter numbering systems

Starting at the beginning of the codex, three folios are given folio numbers A, B and C. There follow three folios marked I, II and III. The next folio is then marked iiij, in a hand that will continue to mark most of the folio numbers, at the top right of the recto folio, until 93r. But ff. 5 and 7-10 are marked with the hand that marked ff. 1-3. Ff. 13, 14 and 15 are missing. After f. 93 follow two paper folios, and eleven parchment folios, marked in a new hand in Arabic numerals from f. 94 through f. 106, which is the last in the manuscript. The text of the customs, beginning with the prologue and ending with chapter 57, occupies ff. 17r. to 93v, or 77 folios, written continuously recto and verso.

In a recent article, Jacques Clémens gives the chapter headings of the Stockholm manuscript, and compares them with the chapters of the *Livre Juratoire* and *N*.[34] He notes five parts of the currently known manuscripts:

"I noyau original (38 art) . . .

II 1er enrichissement de l'article 38 (10 art)[35]

III 2e enrichissement de l'article 38 (6 art)

IV 3e enrichissement (5 art) non "officialisé" en 1370[36]

V. Dernier enrichissement (4 art) pour arriver au total de 42 art."

The *Livre juratoire* bears out Clémens's analysis of these parts. I adopt here his numbering system.

Part I (37-38 chapters) begins at f. 17r., after the gospels, the swearing pages and the table of contents, and continues to f. 65v. The last large picture but one (approx–imately 6.5 X 4 cm.) is on f. 63r., between the preamble and the text of chapter 37.

Part II (11 chapters) continues from f. 65v to f. 81r.. There is no discernible change in the handwriting or the style of the initials in this section, compared with the previous one, but it contains only one more large picture. From chapter 38 to chapter 53 (i.e. to the end of Part III), a later hand has added numbers in very small Arabic numerals next to the initial letters of the preambles or the chapter texts. The person doing this recognizes the difference between preamble and text, except at chapter 52-53. Here chapter 53 has been correctly labeled 17 in the series, but afterwards, whether or not by the same hand, a large initial in the middle of chapter 52, of the size that usually marks the beginning of a chapter, has been labeled 17, and at the beginning of chapter 53 the 17 has been changed to an 18. Chapter 54 is also given a number, 39. But this is evidently an error, because chapter 55 is also labeled chapter 39.

---

[34] Clémens, p. 6

[35] Clémens refers to what are called chapters here as "articles." The text itself calls them "capitols."

[36] That is, not appearing in the *vidimé* which was the manuscript prepared when the customs were approved by the Count of Anjou and then the King.

A later hand has added in the margin next to the beginning of chapter 38: De feudis. This section is well labeled in this way, because it contains the feudal law of Agen. In other customaries, such as those of Marmande and Gontaud, a series of 74 articles (chapters) is labeled by Paul Ourliac: "un petit traité de droit foncier"[37] and "un fort remarquable traité de droit féodal."[38]

Part III (six chapters) continues from f. 81r. to f. 91r.. On f. 81r. the handwriting changes. While the number of lines per page (22) does not change, the words are spaced more loosely, so that there are fewer words per page (f. 80v contains 133 words, f. 81v only 107). From f. 81r. also the background of the illustrations changes. Gone are the red and blue squares, replaced by a solid gold background, in the initials. Some large initial letters mark the beginnings of paragraphs, and some very large capitals at the beginnings of chapters are decorated with pieces that include small animals.

Part IV. There is no part IV in this manuscript. However, the five chapters that compose it are included as Appendix B, in a transcription from the Stockholm manuscript.

Part V continues from f. 91v to 93v. The three chapters that form this last part are marked in a later hand 39, 40 and 41.[39] The initial letters of preamble and text, of equal size, are in a slightly different style from all the initials that have gone before. The ink is a different color, and the writing is also somewhat different. The ink and the hand correspond to the entries for the last three chapters in the table of contents, but it is hard to say that the initials do. In the table, only the capital letter L appears, and there is no L among the capitals in the text. The vertical red lines that mark the text space have clearly been added after the text was written in, for the actual guidelines are still visible, and the red lines do not cover them.

Thus the evidence of the manuscript is that there are truly four parts of this text, as identified by Clémens. The first two sections seem to be written by the same hand and decorated by the same decorator. The overall style, however, is that of a de luxe manuscript, with numerous colored illustrations and decorations, legible hands, the inclusion of heavily illustrated gospel sections and a table of contents. This manuscript contains the swearing pages, not found in any of the other manuscripts.

The Noubel manuscript seems to be written in a homogeneous style, in a single hand. The Stockholm manuscript, a more banausic copy, with numerous expunctions and corrections, is also written in a single hand, and contains bourdons that indicate that it is indeed a copy. The *rouleau*, MS A, is self-confessedly a copy of an existing book.

The changes that mark the transitions from one part to another of the *Livre juratoire*, as outlined above, suggest that this was the copy that represented the original core text, subsequently augmented at different times, but with insufficient attention to making the table of contents conform with the rest of the text after part I. It is therefore very tempting to conclude that this is the manuscript from which the others derive for parts I-III and V and the table of contents.

---

[37] Ourliac and Gilles, vol.1, p. 7.

[38] Ourliac and Gilles, vol. 1, p. 49.

[39] The table of contents includes a heading for chapter 42, but there is no text for it. In the table of contents, next to the heading, appears in a much later hand the word: "deficit". After the end of the last chapter of the text, on f. 93v, in the same hand, appear the words "deficit 42."

In addition to the numbering systems described above, it must be noted that from f. 17r. to f. 67r., the recto and verso pages are numbered consecutively from f. 1 to 101. The page numbers appear in the middle of the top of the page. They do not seem to correspond to any particular part of the text. The chapters from 1 to 38 are correctly identified by a small Arabic number next to the initial letter of the chapter. One or two other persons seem to have attempted to number the chapters, with varying, but not great, success. At least one has crossed out some of the numbers placed in the margins by his predecessors. There is confusion about what is a chapter, and some are deceived by the preambles that precede the chapter texts.

B. How MS 42 came about

One can conjecture that at some time there existed a manuscript, including a table of contents, containing thirty-eight chapters, where the last chapter was divided into eleven sections. These eleven sections (Clémens's part II) might have been added to a previous version containing only thirty-seven chapters. This version of 48 chapters was copied into the Bordeaux manuscript, which evolved no further. Three more parts evolved: one containing six chapters, including one chapter on judicial battle and one on notaries' fees (Clémens's part III); another part contained up to five chapters (Clémens's part IV); and finally a part containing three chapters, but four in the table of contents (Clémens's part V). These parts were variously combined in the different extant manuscripts. The *Livre Juratoire* contains all the parts except part IV, but its table of contents includes only the core, ending with chapter 38 (however long the last "chapter" may have been) and numbering the last four chapters in the table of contents 39-42. The table of contents of S includes only thirty-eight chapters, although the text of that manuscript includes all but the last three (or four) chapters. Nevertheless, the headings of the last four chapters have been copied into the table of contents of S in a much later hand, probably from the *Livre juratoire.* Manuscript N includes all the parts, but its table of contents ends at chapter 38. All this suggests that that the *Livre juratoire* may have at some time consisted of Parts I and V, for then the table of contents would have been correct, although part I may have included Part II as a long chapter 38.

Thus while the different manuscripts are composed of different portions of text, the tables of contents reach only chapter 38, except that the table for the *Livre juratoire,* ignoring many chapters in between, lists also the last three (or four) chapters, numbering them 39-42.

The Customs of Montpezat offer a variation. This collection, which clearly derives from the *Costuma d'Agen,* includes most of the chapters in the *Livre juratoire,*[40] three of the chapters in Part IV that are new in mss. N and S, and a chapter added at the beginning of Part II, fixing the size of fiefs. There is an 18th century French translation of this manuscript, the Occitan copy of which ends after the new chapters. The French version includes at the end some chapters of purely local force, concerning, for example, firewood and food. The various sections are numbered differently by the editors, with the Occitan text ending at section 90. However, the editors helpfully provide a concordance with the Moullié edition, which shows that most of the provisions are the same and in the same order.

[40] Missing is chapter 50, the tariff of charges for notarial services.

If it is true that the *Livre juratoire* was written at different times, the problem of dating it becomes more complex. The different parts must be assigned to different dates. All in all it seems plausible that Part I, chaps 1-37, were written some time before the middle of the 13th century. Shortly thereafter, while the same scribe and decorator, and even the illustrator, were still available, chapters 38-48 were added. Some time later, chapters 49-54 were added by a different scribe and illustrator. Finally, the last three chapters were added and the table of contents enlarged. Probably soon after the Agenais and the *Livre juratoire* passed into French hands, the beginning of chapter 2 was obliterated. The attack of the Roman lawyers on customary law was well launched in the 13th century. Charter CXXV, of about 1302, gives an opinion provided by five doctors of law from Toulouse, whose argument is supported only by citations from Roman and Canon Law.[41] It seems less likely that the city and council would be producing a de luxe copy after that time, although the *Livre juratoire* was clearly still in occasional use perhaps as late as the Revolution.

Language of the text

The text of the *Costuma d'Agen*, regardless of the manuscript, is in standard thirteenth-century Occitan prose, except for a few features (for example, the indirect object pronoun, 3d p.s. is *lo*, whereas in standard Occitan it is *li*). There are few dialectal features, few Latinisms (a tendency to use absolute constructions), no Anglicisms. The text often deals with hypothetical or future events, and therefore its use of tenses differs from that of narrative prose, which deals with the past. For example, the *Costuma* uses a high proportion of future tenses, and relatively few past tenses.[42] An interesting feature is the future participle, also used as an adjective and noun (e.g. *avenidors* in the first sentence: "those who will come"). There is some specialized vocabulary, such as the names of barrels used in winemaking (*cubelot, rec*), but the bulk of the lexicon is standard, using words easily found in a dictionary. Pierre Bec names this variety of Old Occitan *l'occitan juridique commun* in its manifestation as the *scripta toulousaine.*[43]

Place in the customary literature

There are other customary texts from the same time and the same area as the *Costuma*. Some of these have been published by Paul Ourliac and Monique Gilles.[44] The *Costuma d'Agen* is longer than some of these texts, but they all contain much the same kind of material, and two of them (from Port Sainte-Marie and Montpezat) were clearly copied in whole or in part from the *Costuma.*[45]

The illustrations, their relation to the text

---

[41] See also Eduard Moritz Meijers, *Responsa doctorum tholosanum* (Haarlem: H. D. Tjeenk Willink, 1938).

[42] See my article "Aspects of Old Provençal (Old Occitan) Syntax: Relative Clauses in the Costuma d'Agen," *Etudes de langue et de littérature médiévales offertes à Peter T. Ricketts*, ed. Dominique Billy and Ann Buckley (Turnhout: Brepols, 2005), pp. 587-594.

[43] Pierre Bec, *Anthologie de la prose occitane du moyen âge*, vol. 2 (Valdariás: Vent Terral, 1987), p. 117.

[44] For a map showing the various customs that derive from the *Costuma d'Agen*, see Ourliac and Gilles, vol. 2, p. 28.

[45] For the law of Montpezat, see Ourliac and Gilles, vol. 2, p. 75.

The principal interest of the *Livre juratoire* as opposed to the other manuscripts, and the editions made from them, lies in its illustrations. Seventeen of these occupy the whole width of the space generally assigned to the written text, and this space is about 6.5 cm wide. Other illustrations are in large capital letters, averaging about 2 cm by 3 cm, but the difference between the two sizes of illustration is that of scope and number of characters portrayed, rather than any difference in the scenes represented. While many of the illustrations seem "generic" showing one or more "judges" or council members sitting on a bench, each shows some relation to the chapter in which it appears. In a chapter on wills, for example, we see a dying man in a bed and a fainting "daughter". In a chapter on measuring land, we see a man carrying a measuring rod and two other men who are probably official witnesses sent to observe the measurement. A few of the pages have marginal decorations, showing the usual assortment of birds and fantastic animals. There seems to be a change in style, possibly of artist, at about f. 81, when the backgrounds of the illustrations change from red or blue squares to gold. Likewise, the style of the initials changes again (they are no longer historiated) at chapter 55. But much remains to be said about the illustrations and their relation to the text. Previous descriptions of the illustrations are often inexact. For example, Rébouis states that they appear at the beginning of each chapter, which is not true. There are but seventeen "large" illustrations. Some chapters have colored initials, without historiation, for example chapter 10 and the last three chapters.

Agen and the Agenais

The city of Agen lies on the right (northern) bank of the Garonne river. The Agenais (the region around Agen), Gascony, the Aquitaine, Armagnac, Guyenne, these are so many regions of southwestern France whose boundaries are often hard to fix, whose frontiers and names change over time, and whose political allegiance in the Middle Ages shifts from France to England and back again.[46] Gascony lies to the south and west of the river Garonne, which flows through or past Toulouse, Agen, La Réole, Marmande and then Bordeaux. While English kings ruled parts of Aquitaine, including Bordeaux, from the twelfth century until 1453, the Agenais on the north bank of the Garonne changed hands a number of times. Part of the Angevin empire of Henry II, acquired through his marriage to Eleanor of Aquitaine, it was given by Richard I Lion Heart to Raymond VI of Toulouse when Raymond married Richard's sister Joan in 1196. The change in the rulers of Agen is inscribed in the pages of the *Livre juratoire* itself: on f. 20v is a statement that the salt trade of Agen was given to King Henry (presumably Henry II of England 1153-89) to finance his wars in the region. This statement has later been inked out (we know what is says from other manuscripts), presumably after one of the times the territory passed back into French hands. The Agenais suffered under Simon de Monfort during the Albigensian Crusade. Simon was

[46] There exists a charter from the king of France, giving the Agenais to England after the treaty of Amiens in 1279, (Charter LX, Magen and Tholin, p. 83) and several marking its transfer to the French crown in the 1290's (Charters LXXXV, XC, and XCIII, Magen and Tholin, pp. 139, 152, 160). See also Yves Renouard, "Les institutions du duché d'Aquitaine des origines à 1453," *Etudes d'Histoire médiévale* (Paris: S.E.V.P.E.N., 1968), pp. 883-910.

even declared Count of Toulouse for a while, and thus the lord of the Agenais. The principal agricultural product of the region, wine, was regulated by customary laws that appear in the *Costuma d'Agen*, as was also the salt trade. Merchants dealing in both these commodities clearly rely on the cheap transportation afforded by the river. Control of the river traffic and tolls levied on goods passing up and down the Garonne led to many disputes between Agen (in the territory of the count of Toulouse) and La Réole (in the territory of the count of Poitiers) in the thirteenth century. Much wine (especially Buzet) is still grown in the region, which is now also famous for its prunes, peaches, melons and garlic, not to mention ducks and geese.

Civic development in Agen

The city government of Agen, as described in the *Costuma*, seems to be largely in the hands of the citizens. Albert Rigaudière notes that in the thirteenth century for a city to be a *communitas* or *universitas* and to enjoy the status of a "bonne ville," it must have certain characteristics: it must be referred to as a *universitas*, it must have a city hall (*maison de commune*), a treasure chest (*arche*), a seal, and a flag. It should be able to raise money for public purposes, and have the power to assemble and deliberate, *consulere*.[47] In the *Costuma*, the word *universitatz* is frequently used (*passim*), the city is said to have a flag (chapter 52 and illustration on f. 18v), and there is a procedure for raising money (chapter 53). But there is no mention in the *Costuma* of a town hall nor a treasure chest, nor a seal, although these things are mentioned in the charters. There clearly was a council (*passim*), which appears to have deliberated at least as a law court (*passim*), and (since we have them) someone must have written down the laws. The council was enabled to enact regulations (the police power, chapter 29), which implies that the council could deliberate as well as sit as a court (chapter 10 and many illustrations). Men could be chosen to enact public business away from Agen, and their expenses were reimbursed out of public funds (chapter 52).

Another stage in the development in southern French cities, the participation of trade guilds in city government, is not apparent in the *Costuma*. Rigaudière sees this movement as gaining strength in the fourteenth century.[48] The chronology of such development in southern France is subject to all sorts of local variations.

The comital or royal administration was trying to wrest jurisdiction from the local authorities in the thirteenth century. The customs say that the seneschal cannot act alone in criminal cases (chapter 16) and the council has to invoke this right in testimony leading to the opinion by the doctors of Toulouse (Charter CXXV), mentioned above. It was one of the most jealously guarded privileges of the council. Another was that the lord had to swear his oath to the citizens and council before they swore to him (chapter 1). The citizens claimed this right on numerous occasions, down to the eighteenth century, as recorded by Moullié.[49]

Much of the law in the *Costuma* is not new. Charters preserved in Agen go back to Richard Lion Heart, who announced rules for the bridge across the Garonne in Agen in

---

47 Albert Rigaudière, *Gouverner la ville au moyen âge* (Paris: Anthropos, 1993), pp. 36-40.
48 Rigaudière, pp. 213-214.
49 Moullié, "Notice," pp. 165-167.

1189.[50] Charter no. XI, given by Raymond VI, count of Toulouse, is perhaps the source for much of the Prologue of the *Costuma*, and for portions of chapter 28, or perhaps it copies them. This charter has been reprinted in the present volume as an appendix, along with Charter XLVI from 1248, which also parallels many of the provisions of the *Costuma*. A reading of these charters shows, among other things, that the *Costuma* itself conveniently codifies much of the law that was already in effect in Agen. The charters also provide information that is missing from the thirteenth-century text of the *Costuma*.[51] For example, the latter does not say that the men of the council are called "consuls," as they are in many southern towns beginning in the twelfth century.[52] However, the charters frequently mention the *consules* of Agen in Latin. The first mention dates from about 1217. Likewise, the charters mention a mayor (*maior*) in Old Occitan in about 1216, and in Latin (*maior*) in 1217, although no such official is named in the *Costuma*.[53] Already in 1212 there is a mention of a Town Clerk (*communis notarius*), a post not mentioned in the *Costuma*.[54] Pope Innocent III mentions the *universita*[*s*] of Agen in 1216, suggesting that already at that time the city was beginning to be emancipated from the lord.[55] The lord is quite frequently mentioned in the *Costuma*, but not by name. The Charters show that Agen had as a lord Richard I Lion Heart of England, then Raymond VI, count of Toulouse, to whom the Agenais passed as a dowry when he married Richard's sister Joan in 1196, and then his son Raymond VII of Toulouse. After Raymond VII's death, the county passed to King Louis IX's brother, Alphonse de Poitiers, who had married Raymond's daughter Joanne, and finally, when Alphonse died in 1271, the title passed to the King of France, Phillip III. As a term of the 1279 Treaty of Amiens, the King of France ceded the Agenais to the King of England.[56] After 1291 it returned to France. Mention of the lord in the *Costuma* must therefore have meant, in practical terms, the seneschal or the *bailli* who administered the city from day to day. A systematic reading of the charters in comparison with the *Costuma* would be rewarding, but is beyond the scope of this Introduction.

The lord's obligations

The lord must swear his oath to be a good lord when he first enters the city, and he must do this before the townsfolk swear loyalty to him. The lord's ability to make war or lay sieges depends on the participation of the townsfolk, but only for a fixed period each year. The lord has the monopoly of the salt trade (not just a salt tax), and is entitled to the loser's horse and armor after a (judicial) duel. But no man of Agen was

---

[50] Charter I, Magen and Tholin, p. 1

[51] There is mention of the consuls in the endpapers of the *Livre juratoire*, but these are clearly from a later period.

[52] André Gouron, "Diffusion des consulats méridionaux et Expansion du droit romain aux XIIe et XIIIe siècles," *Bibliothèque de l'Ecole des chartes* 121 (1963), pp. 26-76.

[53] Charters VI, VII, Magen and Tholin, pp. 8-9.

[54] Charter III, Magen and Tholin, p. 5. This clerk who names himself W. de la Gleiza appears again in about 1218 as W. de Lagleiza, Charter IX, Magen and Tholin, p. 12.

[55] Charter IV, Magen and Tholin, p. 6.

[56] A charter commemorating the handing over of the Agenais to Edward I of England appears as Charter LX, Magen and Tholin, p. 83.

obligated to fight a duel. The lord's obligations include military security of the city (chapter IV and Charter XII of 1221), the punishment of criminals, and judicial service in partnership with the council.

The council

The text offers some details of city life in Agen in the late thirteenth century, although much that we would like to know is omitted. For example, a new arrival as a citizen is exempted from the watch for a year. This is the only mention of the watch,[57] yet clearly the town watch must have been regulated, administered and captained in some way that is not specified elsewhere in the *Costuma*. Customs for wine production concern the timing of imports into Agen, the size of barrels and vats, and the coloring of the results of the harvest with red wine (chapters 54 and 55). These were no doubt important safeguards for wine-producers, but they seem sketchy and insufficient for one of the main industries of the town. It is, of course, possible that the regulation of the wine trade was effected by a trade association, but there is no trace of this in the *Costuma*. More space is devoted to notaries, who clearly have a stake in the codification of their profession, and were probably involved in the writing of the text that regulates their fee scale (chapter 50). It is noteworthy that a picture of a notary shows money changing hands.[58] A town crier was used for official announcements, and could also be hired to advertise businesses (chapter 52). Two trumpeters were also in the pay of the city, and are seen participating in events in some of the illustrations.[59]

It is only to be expected that a good deal of space is devoted to property, its ownership, its measurement, its transfer from one person to another by sale, by lease, and by inheritance. It is hard to know exactly what the status is of landowners, who are referred to as "senher del feus." They may have been mere citizens, rather than noble lords. They could be summoned into the lord's court on which ordinary citizens sat, so that it seems unlikely that these lords of fiefs were noble. Land might be granted subject to feudal service, but it seems that it was usually merely rented. Even rented land was referred to as *feus*, however. Various persons who needed to measure land could hire a person specializing in measurement, who appears in one of the illustrations (chapter 37 and f. 63v).

Legal procedure

Legal procedure is not a preoccupation of the *Costuma*, which deals mainly with substantive law. The law itself is contained in the written text, but can also be ascertained by consulting the city council, or failing that the local citizens (Prologue). Before going to court on a civil matter, a plaintiff first had to seek a settlement with a

---

[57] The last folio of MS S includes in a later hand the names of various district watches, e.g. *de Moncorni* and *de la clauzura*.

[58] F. 82v.

[59] For example on fs. 18v, 42v and 44v.

defendant in most cases, or risk being thrown out of court (chapter 5). The citizens of Agen could not be made to fight judicial duels, but there is also no mention of appeals to anyone beyond the council (chapter 11). The charters show that in some cases citizens appealed all the way to the King.[60] Plaintiffs who brought suits to harass other citizens had to prosecute their suit or desist (chapter 12). There is a chapter on the *garant*, a common figure in thirteenth-century law courts (chapter 13). This is usually the person who can explain the situation, for example when two persons claim to own the same object, one of them may be able to produce in court the person from whom he obtained it and who will thus justify his claim.

It appears from the *Costuma* that there was an ecclesiastical court in Agen, because there is a fee schedule for notaries who appear before it ("*de carta de la tenor sobredicha don cove anar denant l'official.*" chapter 50), and we know from other documents that Agen was the seat of a bishopric. If a church institution acquired some property, it had to be returned to secular hands within a short time (chapter 18). Part of the qualification for being a notary or a city councilor was not being a heretic (chapter 52); but apart from that the church seems to be almost absent from the text of the *Costuma*, and it is not clear that there are illustrations that include clerics.

Crime is not very fully treated in the *Costuma*. Murder, robbery, rape and arson are hardly defined. A man who finds another inside his locked house at night, and kills him when he resists, is not prosecuted (chapter 20). The punishment for using false measures is prescribed, in this commercial city where the regulation of trade is important (chapter 14). Certain offenses such as adultery and false witness are given special prominence, both being illustrated, and each punished by the *course*, where the guilty parties are made to parade through the city so that their status as criminals is made manifest to the community (chapters 19 and 21, and illustrations on ff. 42v and 44v). There is mention of a pillory, although there are no written customs that govern its use, and no illustrations that include it (chapter 52 in a correction). A man could forbid another to come near his wife, and one of the most poignant illustrations shows this happening in front of witnesses (chapter 20 and f. 43v).

The money described in the *Costuma* is measured in liuras, sols, and deners. The mint that produced the coinage was in Agen itself, and its name probably goes back to an eleventh-century bishop Arnaud or Arnald, perhaps Arnaud de Boville (1020-1049), who received the privilege of coining money in Agen.[61] The name of the money is abbreviated, so that a typical fine of 5 sous is noted ".v. sol dar" (with abbreviations marked on the *l* and above the *r*). The name is only once spelled out in full, in connection with the smallest coin, the *mealha arnaldenca,*[62] which permits us to interpret the abbreviation. Other customary texts also refer to this kind of money.[63]

The ordinary citizen of Agen might have recourse to the law if he needed to repudiate the crimes of some member of his household, for the enforcement of wage contracts, or rentals, as well as for the ordinary purposes of suing someone. There were

[60] Charter LXXIII, Magen and Tholin, p.114

[61] Nony, p. 8.

[62] F. 21v, line 3.

[63] Marmande, *arnaldenc,* Art. 16, *ernaudenxs*, Art 17, Ourliac and Gilles, vol. 1, p. 112, etc. See the article by Daniel Nony. MS S spells out the name of the money as *arnaudencs* at the end of chapter 3.

customs to give guidance as to how to declare bankruptcy (chapter 23) and how to form and dissolve partnerships and other business associations (chapter 57).

The bias and completeness of the *Costuma d'Agen*

Depending on the preoccupations of the person writing down the law, any given *coutumier* will have a bias. For example, Part II of the *Etablissements de St. Louis* (the law of the Orléanais) is concerned with establishing royal as opposed to local jurisdiction. Beaumanoir (an active judge) has a great deal to say about the orderly procedure in local courts. The bias in the *Costuma* would seem to be the assertion of the power of the city council, as opposed to that of the lord.

It is characteristic of most customary compilations that they omit a good deal of law. In a sense, it is the interesting exceptions that are recorded in the law books. It is understandable that a problem not encountered in Agen, for example, will not be found in the *Costuma*. Thus, topics such as service horses (*rossin de service*), swarming bees, leper houses, taverns, beached whales, grazing and wood-gathering rights, servitude, the origins of the law, reports of actual trials, the regulation of the width of roads, the names of witnesses to important lawmaking, and generally any mention of individuals, are absent from the *Costuma*, although they may appear in one or more other compilations of laws, and may even form there the subjects of whole chapters.[64] Likewise, certain topics such as adultery, the regulation of floating mills, and a schedule of payments to notaries are present in the *Costuma*, but are not found in other, well-known compilations. Very little space is given to theoretical, speculative or abstract considerations.[65] Technical terms are not explained. There are no sure references to written law (Roman law) nor to any law other than what is in the *Costuma,* although traces of Roman law, or the unwritten customary law of south-west France generally, may be detected. Some customaries cite to Roman law, or incorporate it into customary law, with or without an acknowledgment.[66] The *Costuma d'Agen* is practical law.

Transcriber's/translator's note

The transcription published here was made from a hitherto unpublished manuscript, Agen Archives départementales de Lot-et-Garonne MS 42. It was not available when two previous transcriptions were made, of different manuscripts. It was available to Henry Tropamer, but he chose to edit the Noubel manuscript, recently bought by the former Mayor of Agen, and given to the Bibliothèque municipale d'Agen, because it contained five chapters not present in the *Livre juratoire.* A transcription and translation of these chapters from manuscript S is provided in Appendix B. Only the most recent edition, by Tropamer, is accompanied by a "translation," which is more like a resumé than a translation, whereas the translation provided here is complete.

---

[64] There is no mention of the king, except the once to King Henry II of England, later inked out.

[65] For example, the definition of *justicia* as *drechura* in chapter 15 is not very helpful. Most of the examples of justice in this chapter concern the punishment for various offences.

[66] The compilation called *Etablissements de St. Louis* gives abundant citations but few actual quotes, while Beaumanoir sometimes quotes Roman law but never acknowledges it as a source. De Fontaines and the *Livre de jostice et plet* translate large sections of Roman law.

The task of the present editor and translator was made easier by the existence of these three editions, however, and made even easier by the developments in digital photography, which permitted the making of a complete record of the manuscript, with the permission of the Archives départementales de Lot-et-Garonne, Agen, to whom thanks are due. The digital images thus created could be displayed in the top half of a computer screen, while the transcription could be written on a file in the bottom of the screen. The picture of the manuscript could be manipulated, so as to enlarge the image, or even to enhance colors, etc. The Archives départementales subsequently had the manuscript digitally photographed and posted the images on their web site.

The translation printed here makes no pretence of elegance: it aims to be as faithful as possible to the original Old Occitan text. In most cases, sentences correspond in length between the text and the translation. Where the translator was in doubt, the Old Occitan text was supplied in square brackets, and sometimes a note was added. Round parentheses are used to aid mere comprehension of the text, and the text within is found in the original. The chapter numbering is in broad agreement with that found in the other editions, and is supplied in square brackets and capitals, e.g. [CHAPTER V]. These chapter numberings do not appear in an official way in the *Livre juratoire* but they follow for the most part the chapter numberings in the other printed editions. The folio numbers of the manuscript are indicated in square brackets, and these adopt numbers inscribed on the manuscript, although such numbers are not medieval. The translator's additions to the text are contained in curly brackets. These additions may be clarifications of the text, or disambiguations of pronouns, or alternative readings. I's, j's and u's have been corrected according to modern practice. Endnotes to the text and translation largely concern the deciphering of words in the manuscript, and justification of the translator's choices. In other parts of the book, footnotes are used for convenience. Roman numerals in the text are translated as Arabic numerals, and not spelled out. Some notes refer the reader to an item in the bibliography that gives more information than is justified in a footnote. Readers doubting my transcriptions or eager to see what they represent, can go to the website and see the manuscript for themselves. See p. IXn.

There are a few words that give difficulty throughout the text. The *prozhomes* of the city and the council have here been translated as "goodmen." This somewhat old fashioned word has the advantage of being a near calque of the Old Occitan word, and of being close to it in meaning. A person owning a fief [*feus*], if there could be said to be ownership in Agen, is referred to as *lo senher del feus*, which has been translated as "the lord of the fief," although "owner" might have conveyed the sense. Such an owner was not necessarily, or even perhaps usually, a nobleman. However, the *senher del feus* had civil jurisdiction, could hold hearings on matters pertaining to his *feus*, and could rent it out to other men. The word "fief" has been retained for *feus*, although this should not lead the reader to think that a *feus* in Agen was like a northern French fief.

The geographic references could be confusing: the word *ciutat* refers to a central core of the city, perhaps the area round the cathedral, and the *borcs* are outlying districts, perhaps outside the city walls. Those who live in these areas are called respectively *ciutadas* (with the accent on the last syllable) and *borzes*, with the feminine *borzeza*. When these persons are taken together they are called the *universitat*. The text often distinguishes *ciutadas* and *borzes*, only then to include them as the *universitat* with the same rights and privileges. The text also uses the word *habitant*. The word *vila* occurs

throughout the text, and its meaning is hard to determine. In the later chapters, perhaps reflecting a change in usage and the adoption of a French term, the word appears more frequently, and appears to refer to the city and suburbs without naming both. In chapter L, for example, the text refers to a "borgues de la vila." On the other hand, the old Roman administrative term *villa* refers to a larger district, and this might be the meaning of *vila* in chapter IV, since the text mentions the lord's duties to the city: "devers a la ciutat d'Agen" and a few lines later this entity is again referred to as: "la ciutat e la vila d'Agen avant dicha." One could suppose that the lord's duties included defending more than just the city. Rather than try to solve these questions, the translator has used the words "city," "citizen," "suburb" (whose etymology recommends it), "town," and "bourgeois" (despite the possible anachronism). Let the reader beware.

BIBLIOGRAPHY

Previous editions of the *Costuma d'Agen*

"Coutumes privilèges et franchises de la ville d'Agen," ed. Amédée Moullié, in *Recueil des Travaux de la Société d'Agriculture, Sciences, et Arts d'Agen*, vol. 5 (1850), Agen: Noubel, 1850. Pp 235-343. Downloadable (July, 2008) at: http://gallica.bnf.fr/ark:/12148/bpt6k338355.table

Coutumes d'Agen ed. Henri Barckhausen, in *Livre des coutumes de Bordeaux*. 5 vols. Archives Municipales de Bordeaux. Bordeaux: Gounouilhou, 1890. Vol. 5, pp. 216-269.

La coutume d'Agen, ed. and trans. Henry Tropamer. Thèse pour le doctorat. Bordeaux: Cadoret, 1911.

The *Livre juratoire*, Agen Archives départementales de Lot-et-Garonne MS 42, can be seen (July, 2008) at the web site of the Archives départementales: http://www.cg47.fr/archives/coups-de-coeur/Tresors/tresors-archives.htm

Editions of other customary texts

Giry, Arthur, ed. *Les Etablissements de Rouen; Etudes sur l'histoire des institutions municipales de Rouen, Falaise, Pont-Audemer, Verneuil, La Ro.* 2 vols. Paris: F. Vieweg, 1883-85.

Ourliac, Paul and Monique Gilles, eds. *Les coutumes de l'Agenais.* Publications de la Société d'histoire du droit et des institutions des anciens pays de droit écrit, 11. 2 vols. Vol. 1: *Les coutumes du groupe de Marmande. Marmande, Caumont, Gontaud, Tonneins-dessous, la Sauvetat-du-Dropt.* Montpellier, 1976. Vol. 2: *(Bouglon, Montpezat, Montréal, Outre-Garonne et Bruilhois).* Paris: Diffusion Picard, 1981.

Gilles, Henri, ed. *Les coutumes de Toulouse (1286) et leur premier commentaire (1296).* Toulouse: Recueil de l'Académie de législation, 1969.

Secondary Sources

Akehurst, F. R. P. "Good Name, Reputation and Notoriety in French Customary Law." *Fama: the Politics of Talk and Reputation in Medieval Europe*, ed. Thelma Fenster and Daniel L. Smail. Ithaca and London: Cornell University Press, 2003. Pp. 79-94.

---. "Adultery in Gascony." *De Sens Rassis: Essays in Honor of Rupert T. Pickens.* Amsterdam: Rodopi, 2005. Pp. 1-15.

---. "Aspects of Old Provençal (Old Occitan) Syntax: Relative Clauses in the *Costuma d'Agen.*" *Etudes de langue et de littérature médiévales offertes à Peter T. Ricketts*, ed. Dominique Billy and Ann Buckley. Turnhout: Brepols, 2005. Pp. 587-94.

Andrieu, Jules. *Bibliographie générale de l'Agenais et des parties du Condomois et du Bazadais incorporées dans le département du Lot-et-Garonne.* 3 vols. Paris, Agen, 1886-1891.

Andrieu, Jules. *Histoire de l'Agenais.* 2 vols. Paris: Picard; Agen: Ferran, 1893.

Babinet de Rencogne and Moulenq. *Le livre juratoire de Beaumont en Lomagne.* Montauban, 1888.

Barrère, Abbé Joseph. *Histoire religieuse et monumentale du diocèse d'Agen, depuis les temps les plus reculés jusqu'à nos jours.* 2 vols. in 1. Agen: Achille Chairou, 1855-56.

Baumont, Stéphane. *Histoire d'Agen.* Toulouse: Privat, 1991. Pp. 59-67, 82-86.

Bellecombe, André de. *Histoire du château, de la ville, des seigneurs de Montpezat et de l'abbaye de Pérignac.* Auch: Cocharaux, 1898.

---. *Aide-mémoire pour servir à l'histoire de l'Agenais.* Auch: Cocharaux, 1899.

Bisson, Thomas N. "The General Court of Agenais in the Thirteenth Century." *Speculum* 36 (1961). Pp. 254-81.

---. *Assemblies and Representation in Languedoc in the Thirteenth Century.* Princeton: Princeton University Press, 1964.

Bourg, A du. *Etudes sur les coutumes communales du Sud-Ouest de la France.* Paris, 1882.

Bruna, Denis. *Piercing: sur les traces d'une infamie médiévale.* Paris: Textuel, 2001.

Castaing-Sicard, Mireille. *Monnaies féodales et circulation monétaire en Languedoc.* Toulouse: Association Marc Bloch, 1961.

Clémens, Jacques. "L'espace coutumier d'Agen au Moyen Age." *Revue de l'Agenais* 109 (1982). Pp. 3-19.

Cuttino, G. *Le livre d'Agenais.* Cahiers de l'Association Marc Bloch de Toulouse; Documents d'Histoire Méridionale, 1. Toulouse: Centre Régional de Documentation Pédagogique, 1956.

Derrer, Felix. *Lo Codi. Eine Summa Codicis in provenzalischer Sprache aus dem XII. Jahrhundert. Die provenzalische Fassung der Handschrift A (Sorbonne 632). Vorarbeiten zu einer kritischen Textausgabe.* Zürich: Juris Druck + Verlag, 1974.

Devic, Cl. and J. Vaissette. *Histoire générale de Languedoc.* 12 vols. Toulouse: Privat, 1885.

Domengie, Yvonne. "Les causes de la fondation de nos bastides agenaises." *Revue de l'Agenais* 47 (1920). Pp. 260-279, 360-368; 48 (1921) 25-42, 111-122, 183-198, 244-271.

Ducom, André. "La commune d'Agen. Essai sur son histoire et son organisation, depuis son origine jusqu'au traité de Bretigny." *Recueil des travaux de la Société d'agriculture, sciences et arts d'Agen,* 2nd series, 11 (1889), pp. 159-322; 12 (1890), pp. 133-322. Available at: http://gallica.bnf.fr/scripts/catalog.php?IdentPerio=NP00267.

Ducros, Jacques and Louis Esparbez de Lussan d'Aubeterre. *Réflexions singulières sur l'ancienne coutume de la ville d'Agen.* Agen: Gayau, 1665.

Gilles, Henri. "Les livres juratoires des consulats languedociens." *Cahiers de Fanjeaux* 31 (1996) 333-354.

Gouron, Marcel. *Les chartes de franchises de Guienne et Gascogne.* Catalogue des chartes de franchises de la France. Paris: Sirey, 1935

Hollyman, K. J. *Le développement du vocabulaire féodal en France pendant le haut moyen-âge; essai sémantique.* Geneva: Droz, 1957.

Labenazie, Bernard, Darribeau de Lacassagne and vicomte Antoine Godefroy de Dampierre. *Histoire de la ville d'Agen et pays d'Agenois.* Saint-Nicolas-de-la-Balerme: Anna Barrès, 1888.

Lauzun, Philippe. "Le livre juratoire des consuls d'Agen," *Revue de l'Agenais* 37 (1910), pp. 385-394. Offprints were printed by: Agen: Maison d'édition et imprimerie moderne, 1910.

Magen, A[dolphe] and G[eorges] Tholin. *Archives municipales d'Agen. Chartes. Première série (1189-1328).* Villeneuve-sur-Lot: X. Duteis, 1876.

Marboutin, J. R. "La Sauvetat-de-Savères." *Revue de l'Agenais* 28 (1901), pp. 158-178, 236-266, 347-366, 459-468.

Mateu, André. "Une charte capitale pour l'histoire de la société urbaine du Moyen Age." *Revue de l'Agenais* 104 (1977), pp. 263-276.

Michaud-Quentin, *Universitas: expression du mouvement communautaire dans le moyen-âge latin.* Paris: 1970.

Moullié, Amédée. "Notice sur les divers exemplaires manuscrits des coutumes de la ville d'Agen." *Recueil des travaux de la Société d'agriculture, sciences et arts d'Agen.* 6 (1853), pp. 154-180.

---. "Coutumes de Laroque-Timbaud." *Revue historique de droit français et étranger* 10 (1864), pp. 141-194, 391-415; 11 (1865), pp. 73-94.

Nony, Daniel. "La monnaie arnaudine; essai de numismatique." *Annales du Midi* 71 (1959), pp. 5-20.

Ourliac, Paul. "Formation du droit de la France méridionale." *Boletin da Faculdade de Direito* (*Coimbre*) (1961), pp. 5-18.

---. "Les coutumes de Toulouse." *Journal des savants.* (Sept.-Dec. 1970), pp. 213-217. Review of Gilles, see above under Editions of other customary texts.

---. "Les coutumes de l'Agenais." *Annales du Midi* 74 (1962), pp. 241-253.

---. "Note sur les coutumes successorales de l'Agenais." *Mélanges Aug. Dumas.* Annales de la Faculté de droit d'Aix-en-Provence, 1950.

Rébouis, Hippolyte. "Les coutumes de l'Agenais: Monclar, Monflanquin, Saint-Maurin." *Nouvelle revue d'histoire de droit français et étranger* 14 (1890), pp. 387-432.

Rigaudière, Albert. *Gouverner la ville au moyen âge.* Paris: Anthropos, 1993.

Roques, P. "Note sur l'origine de la course." *Revue historique de droit français et étranger* 37 (1959), pp. 398-406.

Simon, Pierre. "Chartes de coutumes de l'Agenais." *Revue de l'Agenais* 133 (2006), pp. 519-541.

Structures sociales de l'Aquitaine, du languedoc et de l'Espagne au premier âge féodal, ed. Philippe Wolff and Jean Schneider. Paris: Editions du CNRS, 1969. Also published in *Annales du Midi* 80 (Oct.-Dec. 1968), pp. 353-624.

FRONT MATTER FROM MS 42.

[f. Ar][1] Livre & Statuts & Coutumes de La Ville D'agen Ecrits & imprimés sur parchemin, Contenant Centquatre feuilles en Tout.

S'étant élevé en l'année 1726 certaines discutions entre Mrs Les consuls, Relativement aux Elections consulaires et parvenues a Mr de Boucher Intendant de la province celui cy afin d'en arreter les progrés, fit rendre un arret au Conseil qui le deputa pour etre prezent, (a,) la jurade assemblee, a l'Election consulaire de la ditte année.

En Execution de cet arret, le Seigneur intendant se rendit au presant autel de ville le 4 8bre de la ditte année, ou en sa presence et celle de la jurade duement convoquée, l'Election fu faitte par les consuls en place

Cette operation faitte, il fût propozé par le Seigneur Intendant a la Jurade assemblée, que pour obvier aux plaintes, & aux murmures, qui lui etoient journellement portés, a raison du nombre des privilegiés que l'election annuelle de six nouvaux Consuls ocazionnoit il ne seroit point expediant de le diminuer En mettant les ellections consulaires a l'instar de celles de la ville de Bordeaux. [f. Av] La jurade ayant delibere sur la proposition et unanimement accquiessé, elle pria le Seigneur intendant de vouloir solliciter un arret au conseil qui autorisat Mrs les consuls pour cette assimilation, la jurade ayant Jugé a propos de faire connoitre au Seigneur intendant, en vertu de quel Titre, Mrs les jurats ou conseillers de Ville jouissoi[e]nt des privileges, il lui fût prezanté les lettres patantes de Louis 13 qui en font mention et lecture prise, il convint qu'on ne pouvoit y porter atteinte que c'etoit des privileges exclusifs a tous autres, il Exhorta cependant Mrs Les consuls a tenir la main a ces lettres patantes et de ne poin(t) permettre que ceux qui ne jouissent point de ces privileges, s'en decorassent, sous pretexte de Certaines Exemptions personnelle(s) a quoi les consuls lui promirent d'estre surveillants.

Apres l'obtantion de l'arret du conseil qui fut prompte, l'Election consulaire fut faitte pour l'année 1727 dans l'ordre suivant.

Les six consuls en place s'assemblerent et nommerent Trois d'entre eux qui resterent pour exercer la dite année 1727 et qui occuperroit les trois premieres places, et Ensuitte il en fût Elû trois nouvaux qui occuperent les trois dernieres places, scavoir Mrs Dortis de boissonade Sanguede avocat et Laclaverie neg/t.

Ayant eté procedé a une nouvelle Election pour l'année 1728, les Trois premiers consuls sortirent, les trois derniers monterent aux Trois premiere[s] places et Mrs Lacepede Ecuyer, Sabatery Florimon avocat & Dupau de labernede, anciens jurats furent Elus.

Le Rang, et la marche des consuls observée dans tous les tems Est que le premier consul a la droite le second a la gauche du premier le Troisieme a la droitte (d)apres le premier le quatrieme a la gauche apres le second et dememe pour les deux autres au Rang de leur nomination. & (?)

[1] This is a transcription (and occasionally abridgment in the portions of the mansucript that precede and follow the text of the customs) of the *Livre juratoire*, namely Agen Archives départementales de Lot-et-Garonne MS 42. The text of the customs proper begins at f. 17r and ends at f. 93v. This is preceded by a table of contents, some extracts from the gospels, etc. starting at f. 1v. At the back of the book is a copy of the confirmation of the customs in Latin, which has been transcribed here, and some lists of city councillors, which have not been transcribed.

Comments of a codicological nature are all suppressed except folio numbers, but see Appendix C. As appropriate, u is changed to v and i to j and vice-versa. In *iutiar, iutie,* etc. the ti is changed to tg as in *iutgar*, etc. in conformity with the manuscript which has *iutgar* etc. when not *iutiar*. This spelling for *iutgar* etc. is shared with the Manuscripts of *Lo Codi*, and probably has a phonetic significance, so it has been retained here.

[f. Br] Le presen livre des coustumes de la ville d'Agen a este relyé de nouveau l'annee mil six cens trente trois estans consuls Messieurs de lefuivre Baulac Dolai depoussou de consisat & Ivelauria et au fon d'icellui est escript le Foullu de Messieurs les Jurats de la dite ville Au soin Deuran Ce jour d'huy le vingt troisieme du mois de decembre an susdit 1633
Le Prezant Livre a eté Relié de nouvau L'année mille sept cents soixante douze par Boé Relieur & ce par les soins de Mr Laclaverie Doyen
[f. Bv] Nothing legible. This page has been pumiced. Several lines have been drawn horizontally across the page as if to mark divisions, and the top few lines have been crossed diagonally as if to cross out.

[f. Cr] Nothing legible on this page. At the bottom of the page in the middle a mark may be the number 2.

[f. Cv] Catalogue de Mrs les jurats l'an 1770
Messieurs
LaClaverie neg/t Doyen
[nineteen other names with professions (mix of ecuyer, médecin, négociant, procureur, avocat)]
[f. 1r] [Twenty-two other names with professions (same mix). List does not fill the page. Written on palimpsest. No. "1" in top right corner.

[The medieval TABLE OF CONTENTS and FACING PAGE TRANSLATION into English begins on page 4-5]

[f. 1v] [MEDIEVAL TABLE OF CONTENTS]

Lo prumers capitols contengutz el prologue parla cum lo cosselhs d'Agen, o .xii. proshomes de bona fama de la meissa ciutat si cosselh no i avia, devo estre creut sober las costumas d'Agen.

Lo segonts capitols parla cum lo senher deu jurar, e cum home d'Agen devo jurar a lui.

Lo ters capitols parla en qual [f. 2r] manera home d'Agen devo far ost al senhor.

Lo quarts capitols parla cum home d'Agen dero al senhor lo sali, e las punheras, e·l mezurage del blat, e alcus diners els molis de Garona.

Lo quints capitols parla de la costuma del sali quals es.

Lo seizes capitols parla cum hom deu enquerre son vezi d'Agen avant que s'en clame al senhor, ne en qual manera se devo menar plags de deutes e de covents denant lo senhor.

Lo setes capitols parla cum negus hom no pot re proar contra home d'Agen si no i avia testimonius d'Agen.

L'oches capitols parla de tota demanda que hom fassa a home d'Agen dont lo senher aia clam,[f. 2v] e tota demanda que·l senher fassa a home d'Agen, ont deu estre plageada e termenada.

Lo noes capitols parla ont se deu proar gras de parentat sobre dreghs de successios e d'escaensas.

Lo dezes capitols parla dels clams qui veno denant lo senhor, en qual manera lo senher o deu far, e cum las principals personas

L'onzes capitols parla cum hom pot apelar al cosselh d'Agen sobre grevaments faghs en jutgament.

Lo dozes capitols parla que deu estre d'ome qui a tort metra autre em plaghs per lui tribalhar.

Lo tretzes capitols parla en [f. 3r] qual manera hom deu traire garent, ni quants dias ne deu hom aver, e cum lo garents o deu far.

ENGLISH TRANSLATION

[f. 1v][1] The first chapter contained in the prologue tells how the council of Agen, or twelve good men of the same city if there should be no council, must be believed concerning the customs of Agen.

The second chapter tells how the lord should swear the oath, and how the men of Agen must swear the oath to him.

The third chapter tells how [f. 2r] the men of Agen must form the lord's army.

The fourth chapter tells how the men of Agen gave to the lord the salt trade, and portions {of milled grains}, and the measurement of wheat, and some dues from the mills on the Garonne.

The fifth chapter explains the nature of the customary law of the salt trade.

The sixth chapter tells how a man must try to settle with his neighbor in Agen before he makes a complaint to the lord, and the way in which suits on debts and contracts must be prosecuted before the lord.

The seventh chapter tells how no man can prove anything against a man of Agen unless there were witnesses from Agen.

The eighth chapter tells where any suit brought against a man of Agen over whom the lord has jurisdiction, [f. 2v] and all suits that the lord might bring against a man of Agen, must be pleaded and come to a result.

The ninth chapter tells where degrees of kinship should be proved, in matters of the rights of direct and lateral succession.

The tenth chapter tells of the suits that come before the lord, how the lord should proceed, and how the principal parties should prosecute the suit, and how inspections of land and counter inspections should be performed.

The eleventh chapter tells how you can appeal to the Council of Agen concerning injuries [*grevaments*] made in a court.

The twelfth chapter tells what should be done with a man who sues another wrongfully in order to harrass him.

The thirteenth chapter tells [f. 3r] how a man may vouch a warrantor, and how many court dates a man can have, and what the warrantor should do.
Lo quatorzes capitols parla de las mezuras d'oli, e de las liuras, e dels marcs, e de las pezas, e de las canas ab que hom cana los draps.

---

[1] The folio numbers correspond to the folios of the MS. as noted also in the Old Occitan transcription.

Lo quatorzes capitols parla de las mezuras d'oli, e de las liuras, e dels marcs, e de las pezas, e de las canas ab que hom cana los draps.

Lo quinzes capitols parla dels laironessis, qual pena ne deu hom passar qui panara l'autrui causa, segont la manera del laironessi.

Lo setzes capitols parla de plagas e de murtres.

Lo dezesetes capitols parla cum se devo far inquisitios sobre murtres, e laironecis, e autras malas fachas.

Lo dezeoches capitols parla d'encorrements que veno en la [f. 3v] ma del senhor per alcus forsfaghs a Agen, qual feuzater lo senher deu metre el feus que l' encorreguts tenga d'alcu a feus, e en qual termeni lo senher deu aver vendut o mes en autra ma aquel feus.

Lo dezenoes capitols parla dels adoltres, qu'en deu estre faghs quant son pres en adulteri.

Lo vinches capitols parla si hom troba home denoghs enclaus en sa maio, o si li trobava de dias despoiss que lo agues defendut.

Lo .xxi. capitols parla de testimonis fals, qu'en deu estre [faghs].

Lo .xxii. capitols parla cum hom pot dezemparar sa molher, o son filh, o home o femna de sa mainada per qualque forfaghs, e qual jurisdictio hom a sobre sa [f. 4r] mainada.

Lo .xxiii. capitols parla d'ome qui deu deute e se reclama per no poder, qu'en deu estre faghs.

Lo .xxiiii. capitols parla d'ome qui empenha maio o autra heretat a son creedor en ma de senhor de feus, dont l'aia dat poder de vendre o d'enpenhar, qu'en deu estre faghs, si amonestats de son creedor autrejar no o vol.

Lo .xxv. capitols parla cum negus hom d'Agen no es tenguts ni deu autrejar maio, ni terra, ni autra heretat que hom tenga de lui a feus, a gleia, ni a maio d'orde, ni de religio, ni a clerc, ni a cavoer, ni a jueu, e si o fazia, e en qual que manera neguna possessios que hom tenga d'alcu ciutada o borzes d'Agen a feus avenia a maio d'orde, o de religio, [f. 4v] o ad alcuna de las personas sobre dichas, parla lo meiss capitols quals costuma n'es.

The fourteenth chapter tells about the measurement of oil, and the liura (pound), and the mark, and weights, and the measures with which cloth is measured.

The fifteenth chapter tells about thefts, what the punishment should be for taking another person's property, according to the nature of the theft.

The sixteenth chapter tells of wounds and murder.

The seventeenth chapter tells how trials for murder and theft and other serious crimes should proceed.

The eighteenth chapter tells of seizures of property which come to [f. 3v] the lord because of crimes in Agen, what sort of fiefholder the lord must place in a fief that the person from whom the seizure was made held from some lord, and the time by which the lord must have sold this fief or transferred it to some one else.

The nineteenth chapter tells of adulterers, and what should be done with them when they are taken in adultery.

The twentieth chapter tells of {what should be done} if a man finds another man locked in his house at night, or if he found him by day after he had forbidden him to enter.

The 21st chapter tells what should be done about false witnesses.

The 22nd chapter tells how a man can disclaim responsibility for his wife or his son, or a man or woman of his household, for some misdeed, and what jurisdiction a man has over his [f. 4r] household.

The 23rd chapter tells of what should be done about a man who owes a debt and says he cannot pay.

The 24th chapter tells {what should be done about} a man who, as a security to his creditor, hands over a house or some other property into the hands of his lord (to whom he has give the power to sell it or use it as a security), and who, when his creditor has given him notice, refuses to hand it over.

The 25th chapter tells how no man of Agen is required to, nor should, hand over a house, or land, or other real property that is held from him as a fief, to any church or to a house belonging to an order or a religious organization, nor to a clerk or a knight or a jew; and if he should do so, and however property held from a citizen or bourgeois of Agen came into the possession of a house of an order, or a religious organization, [f. 4v] or of any of the above-mentioned persons, this same chapter tells what the custom is concerning it.

Lo .xxvi. capitols parla de presomptio per longa tenezo de temps.

Lo .xxvii. capitols parla de causas dadas en dot quals costuma n'es.

Lo .xxviii. capitols parla cum lo senher no deu traire ostatges, ni demandar d'Agen, ni prendre senes jutgament ciutada ni borzesd'Agen, ni deu far castel a Agen, e cum home d'Agen son frang a La Fots, e per tota la terra de la senhoria de Bovi(n)la, e cum devo passar de peatge a Marmanda.

Lo .xxix. capitols parla qual franqueza a lo cosselh d'Agen de far establiments entre ·ls habitants del meiss loc.

[f. 5r] Lo .xxx. capitols parla cum hom pot logar sa maio a Agen e de la costuma del loguer.

Lo .xxxi. capitols parla qual poder lo cosselhs d'Agen a de destrenher tot ciutada o borzes d'Agen de pagar a so sirvent o a sa sirventa son loguer e sa soudada.

Lo .xxxii. capitols parla cum tots ciutadas o borzes d'Agen pot far bastida en sa proprietat.

Lo .xxxiii. capitols parla dels avenediss qui veno de foras per estar a Agen, quals costuma n'es.

Lo .xxxiiii. capitols parla de testaments e dels heretatges dels enfants.

Lo .xxxv. capitols parla dels dreghs de veuzas, e d'orfanhols, e de menors d'etat, [f. 5v] qual razo an a demandar lor dreghs.

Lo .xxxvi. capitols parla si hom venia contra causa jutgada per lo cosselh d'Agen.

Lo .xxxvii. capitols parla de la mezura que hom apela perja, ab que hom perja terra a Agen, quals costuma n'es.

Lo .xxxviii. capitols parla dels dreghs que li senhor dels feus an en lors feus, ni per razo de lors feus, e de las costumas dels feus, quals son en divers capitols conseguentre l'un apres l'autre.

The 26th chapter tells of a presumption {of ownership} because of long tenure {of property}.

The 27th chapter tells what the custom is concerning property given in dowry.

The 28th chapter tells how the lord may not take or demand hostages from Agen, nor arrest a citizen or bourgeois of men of Agen are free of dues at La Fots, and throughout the land of the lordship of Boville, and what tolls they must pay at Marmande.

The 29th chapter tells what power the council of Agen has to make regulations among the inhabitants of the said place.

[f. 5r] The 30th chapter tells how a man may rent his house in Agen, and the custom of rentals.

The 31st chapter tells what power the Council of Agen has to compell every citizen or bourgeois of Agen to pay his employee, man or woman, his or her stipend or salary.

The 32nd chapter tells how any citizen or bourgeois of Agen can build a bastide on his property.

The 33rd chapter speaks of what the custom is concerning newcomers who come from elsewhere to settle in Agen.

The 34th chapter tells of wills and the inheritance of children.

The 35th chapter tells of the rights of widows and orphans and minor-age children, [f. 5v] what grounds they have for suing for their rights.

The 36th chapter tells {what happens} if a man goes against a judgment given by the council of Agen.

The 37th chapter tells what the custom is concerning the measure called a perch, with which land is measured in Agen.

The 38th chapter tells of the rights that lords of fiefs have in their fiefs, or by reason of their fiefs, and what are the customs of fiefs, {which are discussed} in several chapters following one after another.[2]

---

[2] After this point in the medieval table of contents, the chapter numbers in the table of contents and those in the text cease to correspond. The text contains several chapters on fiefs, then more chapters on various topics down to chapter 54. Chapters 39-41, as enumerated in the table of contents, correspond to chapters 55-57 of the text, and chapter 42 as noted in the table of contents (which would have been Chapter 58) is missing entirely from the text. It would have presumably come last in the present compilation, following chapter 41 (here 57), and might have been lost with the last folio or folios of another manuscript. But the text of the customs in manuscript 42 ends part way down a verso page, the rest of the page being filled with the beginning of the Latin text of confirmation given in 1369. Someone who has read the table of contents has written in the margin, at the end of the text on f. 93v, "Chap 42 deficit" 'Chapter 42 is missing.' This chapter

Lo .xxxviiii. capitols parla de la costuma del vi e de la vendenha.

Lo .xl. capitols parla que li senhor d'Agen no devo prendre borzes ni borzeza d'Agen.

[f. 6r] Lo .xli. capitols parla dels captals, e de las cumpanhias, e de las comandas.

Lo .xlii. capitols parla de la franquessa de la ciutat d'Agen, de la crida que hom fa en la feira e en las vendenhas.[3]

[End of the medieval table of contents]

---

is not found in any of the extant (or lost) manuscripts. Yet the chapter heading appears also in the table of contents of N and S.

[3] The chapter enumerated here is missing in the text, and is not found in any other manuscript.

The 39th chapter {here 55th} tells of the custom of wine and the wine harvest.

The 40th chapter {here 56th} tells that the lords of Agen may not arrest bourgeois men or women of Agen.

[f. 6r] The 41st {here 57th} chapter tells of partnerships and business associations and limited partnerships.

The 42nd chapter {missing from the text} tells of the freedom of the city of Agen, and the public announcement that is made on holidays and during the wine harvest.

CONTINUATION OF FRONT MATTER

[f. 6v] Pumiced page, nothing readable.

[f. 7r] Pumiced page, nothing readable. Has been mended with an inferior piece of vellum, which forms about the right hand third of the page.

[f. 7v] Much defaced left hand page of SWEARING PAGE. Picture Of God the Father supporting a crucified Son.

[f. 8r] Much defaced, mended, torn, right hand page of SWEARING PAGE. Shows the Virgin with Christ on her lap.

[f. 8v] More or less blank page. Some paint has come through from 8r. Small patch near left hand edge.

[f. 9r] More or less blank palimpsest. Has large IX in top right corner corner, and trace of the older ix of the usual numerator's hand.

[f. 9v] More or less blank palimpsest. The X of the Xr page has left a mark in the top left hand corner.

[f. 10r] [Portions of Gospels.]

Initium sancti evangelii secundum Johannem.[4]

(1) In principio erat verbum, et verbum erat apud deum, et Deus erat verbum.
(2) Hoc erat in principio apud Deum.
(3) Omnia per ipsum facta sun, et sine ipso factum est nichil, quod factum est.
(4) In ipso vita erat, et vita erat lux hominum,
(5) et lux in tenebris lucet, et tenebre eam [f. 10v] non comprehenderunt.
(6) Fuit homo missus a Deo cui nomen erat Johannes.
(7) Hic venit in testimonium, ut testimonium perhiberet de lumine, ut omnes crederent per illum.
(8) Non erat ille lux, sed ut testimonium perhiberet de lumine.
(9) Erat lux vera, que illuminat omnem hominem venientem in hunc mundum.
(10) In mundo erat, et mundum per ipsum factus est, et mundus eum non cognovit.
(11) In propria venit, et sui eum non receperunt;
(12) quotquot autem receperunt eum, dedit eis potestatem filios Dei fieri, his, qui credunt in nomine ejus:
(13) qui non ex sanguinibus, neque ex voluntate carnis, neque ex voluntate viri, sed ex Deo nati sunt.
(14) Et verbum caro factum est, et habitavit inter nobis: Et vidimus gloriam ejus, gloriam quasi unigeniti a Patre, plenum gratie et veritatis.

[4] This passage is taken from the beginning of the Gospel of John, Verses 1-14. The transcriptions of the Gospels have been given a modern spelling, and capital letters in the modern style. There are few capitals in the manuscript versions.

[f. 11r] Secundum Lucham[5]

In illo tempore: (21) postquam consummati sunt dies octo, ut circumcideretur puer, vocatum est nomen eius Jhesus, quod vocatum est ab angelo, prius quam in utero conciperetur.

[f. 11v] Secundum Matheum.[6]

In illo tempore: (46) loquente Jehu ad turbas, ecce, mater eius et fratres stabant foris, querentes loqui ei.
(47) Dixit autem ei quidam: Ecce, mater tua et fratres tui foris stant querentes te.
(48) At ille [Vulg. ipse] respondens dicenti sibi, ait: Que est mater mea, et qui sunt fratres mei?
(49) Et extendens manum in discipulos suos, dixit: Ecce mater mea, et fratres mei.
(50) Quicumque [f. 12r] enim fe[cer]it[7] voluntatem Patris mei, qui [i]n celis est, ipse meus frater, (et) soror, et mater est.

Secundum Marchum[8]

In illo tempore: Dixit Jhesus discipulis suis. (33) Vigilate et orate: nescitis enim, quando tempus sit.
(34) Sicut homo, qui peregre profectus reliquit domum suam, et dedit servis suis potestatem cujusque operis, et janitori precepit, ut vigilet.
(35) Vigi- [f. 12v] -late ergo (nescitis en[i]m[9] quando dominus domus veniat, sero, an media nocte, an galli cantu, an mane),
(36) ne, cum venerit repente, inveniat vos dormientes.
(37) Quod autem vobis dico, omnibus dico: Vigilate. |

[NOTA BENE. The manuscript has no ff. 13, 14 or 15.]

[f. 16r] More or less blank page (palimpsest)

[f. 16v] More or less blank page (palimpsest)

---

5 The passage is from Luke, Chapter 2, verse 21.

6 This passage is taken from Matthew Chapter 12, verses 46-50. Verse 46 commences in the Vulgate: Adhuc eo loquente ad turbas... and continues as the Agen text.

7 Here a fold in the vellum obscures (probably) the letters *cer* in the word *fecerit*, and in the line below the letter *i* in *in*, and in the same line partly obscures the second letter *o* in *soror*.

8 This passage is taken from Mark, Chapter 13, verses 33-37. Verse 33 begins: Videte, vigitalate, et orate ...

9 A fold in the vellum obscures the letter *i* of *enim*.

OLD OCCITAN TEXT AND FACING PAGE ENGLISH TRANSLATION OF

THE *COSTUMA D'AGEN*

[f. 17r] [BEGINNING OF THE CUSTOMARY PROPER]

In nomine patris et filii et spiritus sancti amen.

[PROLOGUE]

Incipit prologus.[1]

Conoguda e manifesta causa sia a tots los presents e als avenidors, que las costumas e las franquessas d'Agen de la ciutat e dels borcs ancianament aprobadas son escriutas en aquest libre. E si sobre las costumas de la meissa ciutat [f. 17v] se movia contrast entre ·l senhor e ·ls ciutadas, o entre ·ls ciutadas e ·ls balles del senhor, lo senher ne deu creire los .xii. proshomes del cosselh del meiss loc, o si cosselh no ·i avia, deu ne creire .xii. proshomes del meiss loc, que sio de bona renomnada, sobre lor sagrament, que aiso que ilh autregeran que sia costuma lo senher o deu creire, e autrejar, e o deu tener per ferm per si e per tots los seus per tots temps.[2]

[CHAPTER I]

Primum capitulum.

Quant lo senher ve noelament en la terra, deu jurar primerament,[3] cum senhor, que el [f. 18r] bons senhers e leials sera al cosselh et a tots et a cadau los habitants e habitadors d'Agen, e gardara senes tot enfranhement lors fors, e lors costumas, e lors franquessas, e lors establiments, e lors razos, e lors drechuras cum bos senher, e los gardara de tort e de forsa de si meiss e d'autrui d'ints e de foras per tots locs a son leial poder a bona fe. E aqui meiss faghs lo dighs sagrament, lo cosselhs e tota la universitats de la dicha ciutat e dels borcs d'Agen devo jurar al senhor que ilh lo seran bo, e fiel, e leial e gardaran sa vita, e sos membres, e sa senhoria, e sas drechuras a lor leial poder a bona fe, salb lors custumas, e los {*sic*} franquessas, e lors establiments. E si lo senher vol far senescalc en Agenes, aquel senescalc [f. 18v] deu jurar primerament al cosselh d'Agen, per lor e per tota la universitat de la meissa ciutat e dels borcs d'enviro, e ·l cosselhs d'Agen deu jurar apres al senescalc per lor e per tota la universitat del meiss loc. E la forma del segrament es aitals cum es dighs desobre del segrament del senhor. E si lo senescalc vol metre balle a Agen, aquel balles deu jurar al cosselh per lor, e per tota la universitat d'Agen, e ·l cosselhs ni li home d'Agen al balle no devo far semblant sagrament ni autre per razo de senhoria. [f. 19r]

[CHAPTER II]

Secundum capitul[u]m.

Li ciutada e li borzes d'Agen devo far ost de .xl. dias continuables al senhor una vets l'an per tot l'ebescat d'Agenes, e deforas lo meiss ebescat si ·l senher ops a, aissi que la meissa noghs que seran issit en ost posco tornar en Agenes, en aital manera

[f. 17r.] In the name of the Father and the Son and the Holy Ghost. Amen.

Here begins the Prologue.[4]

Let it be known and manifested to all those now alive and those to come that the customs and franchises, approved of old, of Agen, the city and the suburbs, are written in this book. And if a disagreement arose about the customs of the said city [f. 17v] between the lord and the citizens, or between the citizens and the lord's *balle*, the lord should take the word of the twelve goodmen [*proshomes*] of the council of the said place, or if there were no council, then he should take the word of twelve goodmen of the said place, men who are of good reputation, on their oath, that what they affirm was the custom, the lord should believe it and affirm it and take it as firm {-ly established law} for himself and for all his men for all time.

[CHAPTER I]

First chapter.

When the lord newly comes into the territory he must first swear as the lord that he [F. 18r] will be a good and fair [*leials*] lord to the council, and to each and every resident residing in Agen and will keep their statutes [*fors*] and their customs and their franchises and their laws [*establiments*] and their causes of action [*razos*] and their rights [*drechuras*] without any infraction as a good lord {should} and will protect them from wrong and from violence [*forsa*] from himself or from others within and without in all places to the best of his ability [*a son leial poder*] in good faith. And when the said oath has been sworn, the council and the whole community [*universitats*][5] of the said city and suburbs of Agen must swear to the lord that they will be good and faithful and loyal to him and will protect his life and limbs and his lordship and his rights to the best of their ability in good faith, saving their customs and their franchises and their laws [*establiments*]. And if the lord wants to appoint a seneschal in the Agen district, that seneschal [F. 18v] shall first swear to the council of Agen, for them and the whole community of the said City and the suburbs around it. And the Council of Agen must swear afterwards to the seneschal for themselves and for the whole population of the said place. And the form of the oath is as is said above concerning the lord's oath. And if the seneschal wants to install a *balle* in Agen, that *balle* must swear to the council, for them and for the whole community of Agen. And the council and the men of Agen are not obligated to make a similar oath nor any other to the *balle* by reason of lordship. [f. 19r]

[CHAPTER II]

Second chapter.

The citizens and bourgeois of Agen must serve in the army [*far ost*] of the lord for forty continuous days once per year, in the whole diocese of Agen, and outside the said diocese if the lord has need of them, such that on the same night that they left as an army they could return to the Agen district. {And this must be done}in

que ·l senher, si hom lo fa tort en Agenes, o defora lo meiss ebescat, deu mandar e far cridar la ost generalment per tot Agenes, e deu far saber a Agen sobre cui volra cavalgar o metre seti. E si en alcu loc d'Agenes vol cavalcar o metre seti, lo cosseilhs tot primerament, avant que home d'Agen isco en ost, deu enquerre lo senhor e ·ls habitants d'aquel loc. E si ·l senher e li habitant d'aquel loc volo far dreghs a esgart del senhor e [f. 19v] de sa cort, lo senhor los deu drech prendre; e home d'Agen d'aqui en la no son tengut ni devo far ost al senhor sobre aquel o aquels, pero que sio en l'ebescat d'Agenes, que, aissi cum predichs es, volran far dreghs a esgart del senhor e de sa cort, la quals corts deu estre dels baros e dels cavers d'Agenes, e dels cosselhs e dels proshomes de la ciutat d'Agen e dels borcs d'Agenes; mas en autre loc que sia fora l'esbescat d'Agenes lo cosseilhs ni home d'Agen no an enquesta. E si, aissi cum desobre es dighs, cove que ·l senher meta seti en alcu loc, deura primerament assetar ab sas gents e deu estar .viij. dias continuables al seti, avant que home d'Agen isco en ost. E si regnet avia el cami, lo senher los deu trametre tants [f. 20r] homes armats ab los quals pusco salvament anar e tornar. Empero cum que la ost fos issida d'Agen e se fos ajustada ab lo senhor, e ·l senhor per acordament o per als avia deliurada sa cocha dints los predighs .xl. dias, d'aqui en la home d'Agen no ·l devo far ost ni cavalgada de tot aquel an. E la ost deu estre aitals que ·l senher del ostal deu anar en ost o ·i deu trametre per si son filh, o son fraire, o son nebot, o son cozij germa, o son cunhat, si ·n a en sa maio, que tenga a son pa, e a so vi, pero que s ... d'ost far. Salb que . . . fanhols ni hom qui aia . . . aqui en sus d'etat, ni qui va en perelinhatge {*sic*}, o en mercadaria, o malautes, {This passage reads as follows in Moullié: "E la ost deu estre aitals que l senher de l'ostal deu anar en ost o i deu trametre per si son filh, o son fraire, o son nebot, o son cosi germa, o son cunhac, si n'a en sa maio que tengua a son pa e a son vi, pero que sia persona d'ost far, salb que veuza, ni orphanols, ni om que aia LXX ans e d'aqui en sus d'état, ni que sia en pegrinage, o en mercandaria, o malautes,"} ni hom qui no tenga ostal a Agen, ni de cui sa moilher [f. 20v] jaga d'efant, no devo far ost ni cavalgada. E si negus hom d'Agen, despuiss que la ost seria issida d'Agen, defailhia que no fos en la ost cumunalment ab la universitat d'Agen, lo senher auria sobre lui .lxv. sols d'arnaldencs de gatge si per razonabla excusacio defendre no s'en podia.

[CHAPTER III]

Tercium capitulum.

Cum lo senher ...d'Agen donet al Rei Henric qui en aquel temps era senher d'aquesta terra ... las grans despensas que fa ... per grants guer- [f. 21r] {This passage reads as follows in Moullié: "Cum lo senhor agues ancianament petitas rendas en Agenes, la universitat d'Agen donet al rei Henric qui en aquel temps era senhor d'aquesta terra, per las grans despensas que fazia en grans guerras"} -ras que avia, sali a Agen, e las punheras, so es a ssaber de cada moli qui mola froment o mestura en Garona, del pont de Merdalo entro al port apelat de l'Ebesque, una punhera d'aital blat cum molra, o froment, o mestura a cada dissapte, si ·l molis o gaanha en la setmana (e si no o gaanha en la setmana, no ·i a re); e .v. sols d'arnaldencs cada an en

such a way that if someone does the lord a wrong in the Agen district or outside said diocese, he should order and publicly announce [*far cridar*] the conscription generally in all the Agen district. And he must announce in Agen whom he wishes to make war on or lay siege to; and if he wants to ride out to or lay siege to some place in the Agen disctrict before the men of Agen go out as an army, the council must first of all attempt a settlement [*enquerre*] with the lord and residents of the said place. And if the lord and residents of the said place are willing to go to court [*far dreghs*] to obtain a ruling from [*a esgart de*] the lord and [f. 19v] his court, the lord should give them a hearing [*drech prendre*]; and from then on the men of Agen are not required nor should they form the lord's army against the man or men (provided they are within the diocese of Agen) who are are willing as before stated to go to court to obtain a judgment from the lord and his court. And the court must be composed of the barons and knights of Agen and the council and the goodmen of the city of Agen and the suburbs of the Agen district. But in any other place outside the diocese of Agen, the council and the men of Agen have no {right to an} attempt at settlement. And if, as is said above, it is necessary for the lord to lay a siege in some place then he must first besiege it with his {own} men and he must be at the siege for eight days continuously with his men before the men of Agen ride out as an army. And if there were to be a danger [*regnet*][6] on the way the lord must send them enough [f. 20r] armed men for them to come and go in safety. However, whenever the troop has left Agen and joined the lord, and the lord, by an agreement or otherwise, has finished his business within the above mentioned 40 days, then from then on the men of Agen are not obliged to form a troop or mounted excursion [*cavalgada*] for the rest of that year. And the troop must be {formed} this way, that the head of the household should form part of the troop, or send in his place his son or his brother or his nephew or his first cousin, or a relative on the male side [*cunhat*] if he has one in his household whom he supports with his own bread and wine (provided he is capable of serving in the troop), except that widowers, and orphans, and men of 70 years of age or more, and those on pilgrimages, or business journeys [*mercandaria*] or who are sick, and a man who has no house in Agen, or whose wife [f. 20v] is in childbirth, are not obliged to form part of the troop or mounted excursion. And once the troop has left Agen, if any man of Agen is missing, so that he is not in the troop with the whole community of Agen, the lord would be entitled to a fine of 75 arnaldenc sous[7] from him, if he could not offer a reasonable excuse in his defense.

[CHAPTER III]

Third chapter.

As the lord formerly had little income in the Agen district, the population of Agen gave King Henry {Henry II of England} who was then lord of this territory, because of the great expenses he had in great wars, [f. 21r] the salt business at Agen and "fractions" [*punheras*]. That is, from each mill that grinds best wheat [*froment*] or mixed wheat [*mestura*][8] on the Garonne, from the Merdalo bridge up to the gate called the Bishop's gate, a "fraction" of the wheat (either best wheat or mixed wheat) that was milled, every Saturday if the mill works during the week. And if the mill does not work that week, there is no payment. And {he gets} 5 arnaldenc sous per year for ev-

cada moli parador que sia en Garona dints los dex avant dichs. E ·l moli que sis dints los dighs dex an estacatge, francament en qual que loc ont no sia [The following three lines read as follows in Moullié: autres molis estacats en qualque loc hom volia mudar son moli dints los meis dex tantas vegadas cum covendra mudar moli] de loc en loc, senes que re n'en deu dar, ni hom vedar no lo deu. E en [f. 21v] cada emina de blat que sera venduda a Agen que sia mezurats, mealha arnaldenca si hom la compra d'un home sol essemps. E si la compra per partidas, que no la compra d'u home sol essemps, lo senher no ·i a re. E de la conqueta de blat que sera venduda a Agen, e mezurada, si hom la compra essemps d'u home sol, .i. diner, e si la compra per partidas, que no la compre essemps d'u home sol, cum que sia cada compra d'emina en aval, no ·i a re lo senher. Pero si no pagava lo dia o l'endema al messatge del senhor lo mezuratge sobredighs quant lo blat auria aissi com predichs es comprat e mezurat, lo senher i auria .v. sols d'arnaldencs de gatge, ont que ·l blats sia mezuratz a Agen. [f. 22r]

[CHAPTER IV]

La costuma del sali es aitals: so es a ssaber que ·l senher pot far pojar lo sali a Agen ab qualsque naus, e ab tantas cum se volra, entro a .xiii. naus, una vets l'an francament, senes peatge que non deu dar en negu loc de sa terra. E tots hom qualsque sia pot pojar sal a Agen en nau. E can sera al port de Moncorni desots los pilars d'Agen, deu la presentar, se vendre la vol, al senhor del sali, so es a ssaber ad aquel qui per lo senhor tendra lo sali, que la compre si comprar la vol. E si comprar no la vol per quant ab lui trobara o autre lu ·n {*sic*} volra dar, pot la aquel qui aportada l'aura estujar a Agen, o vendre, qual que se [f. 22v] voilha, a tot home; pero si la vent o no la vent, el ni aquel a cui la vendra ni autre no pot traire la sal per aga ni per terra d'Agen en fora, senes licentia del senhor del sali. E si o fazia, lo senher del sali i auria .lxv. sols d'arnaldencs de gatge, e la sal encorreguda. Pero si es hom d'Agen, pot ne prendre a son salar, e als uzatges de sa maio, e de son bestiari, e de son bordil si ·n a defora. E si hom nautres o autre qualsque sia dona sal a home d'Agen, pot o far, e d'aquela sal pot se servir l'om d'Agen ops de si, e de sa mainada, e de son bestiari, e de son bordil si ·n a, aisi cum dighs es desobre. Mas si lo senher del sali se cujava que aquel hom d'Agen traisses aquela sal d'Agen, per que la agues dada o [f. 23r] venduda o que la traisses o l'an fes traire per mal genh no pas per sos ops aissi cum dichs es desobre, pot ne aver sagrament d'aquel home d'Agen, si se vol, de vertat que no la aia venduda ni dada ni per autra causa no l'an fasa traire, sino per sos propris ops, o de son bestiari, o de son bordil, aissi cum predighs es. E si lo sagrament far no auzava aissi cum dighs es, lo senher del sali i auria .lxv. sols d'arnaldencs de gatge, e la sal encorreguda. E si alcus hom d'ont que ·s fos volia pojar sal d'Agen ensus en nau en sola, deu s'en acordar ab lo senhor del sali, e puis deu estre la sals mezurada en la meissa nau ont sera al dighs port sots los pilars, e deu la ·n hom traire en sacs quant sera mezurada ab faissers d'Agen, e no [f. 23v] ab autres homes. Li qual faisser devo

ery fulling mill on the Garonne between the two previously mentioned limits. And the mills situated between the said limits have free anchorage in any place where there are no other mills anchored, wherever a man wants to move his mill within the same limits, as many times as he has to move it from place to place, without making any payment, and no man should prevent him. And on [f. 21v] every *emina* of wheat sold in Agen that is measured {there is a tax of} an arnaldenc halfpenny [*mealha*] if it is bought in one lot from a single seller [*d'u home sol essemps*]. And if it is bought in portions, not from a single man in one lot, the lord gets nothing. And for a *conqueta* of wheat that is sold in Agen and measured, if a man buys it in one lot from a single man, {the lord gets} one denier, and if it is bought in portions so that it is not bought in one lot from a single man, provided that [*cum que*] each purchase is one *emina* or less, the lord gets nothing. But if the buyer did not pay the lord's messenger on the same day or the next for the above mentioned measurement, when the wheat was bought and measured as said above, the lord will get 5 arnaldenc sous as a fine wherever the wheat was measured in Agen. [f. 22r]

[CHAPTER IV]

The salt business custom is as follows: it should be known that the lord can have salt brought up to Agen on any ship, and any number of ships he wants up to thirteen, once per year, free of tolls, which he should not pay any place in his territory. And any man whatever can bring salt up to Agen by ship. And when he is in the port of Moncorni, below the pillars [*pilars*] of Agen, if he wants to sell it, he must present it to the salt-lord (that is the man who holds {manages} the salt business for the lord)[9] for him to buy it if he wishes. And if he does not want to buy it for a price he can agree on with him, or another person is willing to give, the person who brought it can store it in Agen or sell it for as much as he [f. 22v] wants to any man; but whether he sells it or not, neither he nor the man he sells it to nor any other man may transport [*traire*] the salt by land or water beyond Agen without the license [*licentia*] of the salt-lord. And if he did, then the salt-lord would get 65 arnaldenc sous as a fine and the salt would be confiscated [*encorreguda*]. But if he is a man of Agen, he can take some for his meat-salting [*salar*] and the use of his household and his livestock [*bestiari*] and his farm [*bordil*] if he has one outside. And if a boatman [*nautres*] or other man whoever he is gives salt to a man of Agen, he can do so, and the man from Agen can use it for his own purpose or for that of his household or his livestock or his farm if he has one, as was said above; but if the lord believed that the man from Agen was transporting that salt from Agen because he had given or [f. 23r] sold it or that he was transporting it or having it transported for a bad purpose [*per mal genh*], and not for his own use as is said above, he can require if he wishes an oath from that man of Agen that he has not sold it nor given it away nor is he having it transported for any other reason than for his own use or for his livestock or his farm as is said above. And if he did not dare swear the oath as said above, the salt- lord gets 65 arnaldenc sous as a fine and the salt is confiscated. And if any man from anywhere wanted to transport salt upstream from Agen by ship in the hold [*en sola*] he must make an agreement with the salt-lord and then the salt must be measured in the same ship where it is at the said port below the pillars, and it must be unloaded into sacks when it has been measured using porters [*faissers*] from Agen and not [f. 23v]

portar tota aquela sal ab sacs de la nau enfora entro ins la porta de Montcorni, e puis devo la ·n tornar aqui meiss li dighs faisser a riba de Garona, e descargar en nau d'Agen que l'an porte d'aqui en sus, e no en autra nau. Pero aquel de cui sera la sals se deu acordar ab los dighs faissers qui la sal portaran, que los ne done lor loguer que ab lor trobara. E si alcus hom portava en nau en sola dels dighs pilars en sus, que no fos mezurada ni portada dedints la dicha porta aissi cum dighs es desobre, lo senher del sali i aura .lxv. sols d'arnaldencs de gatge, e la sal encorsa. E si home d'Agen peciavo aquela nau, podo o far, e non son tengut a senhor ni ad autrui si la pecio. E [f. 24r] neguna naus no deu pojar sal per lo flum d'Out en neguna manera. E si o fazia, la naus e la sals serio encorssas al senhor del sali d'Agen, e auria lo senhor del sali .lxv. sols d'arnaldencs de gatge sobre cada home qui la sal pojario. ¶ Negus hom no deu portar ab bestia ni en neguna manera sal per Gasconha del pont de Barbasta ensus, ni d'Aguilho ensus entre Out e Garona, si del sali d'Agen no la prendia. E si o fazia lo senher del sali i auria .lxv. sols d'arnaldencs de gatge, e la sal e la bestia que la sal portaria encorregudas. Pero tots hom que esto d'outra Garona qui venga al sali d'Agen sal comprar deu aver la sal que volra menhs .xij. deniers d'arnaldencs lo mealha(l) que hom al sali no la vendra. E ·l senher del sali deu gaanhar [f. 24v] en la sal que vendra lo tern diner de tant quant comprada l'aura en sus, e no plus. ¶Item: negus hom ni neguna femna que revendra sal a Agen non i deu mesclar autra mas d'aquela que aura aguda del sali, per so qu'en venda a Agen ni defora. E si o fazia, lo senher del sali auria sobre aquel o aquela .lxv. sols d'arnaldencs de gatge, e la sal encorreguda. E per lo sali avant dighs, e per las punheras, e per lo mezuratge del blat sobredighs, lo senher deu far aquests devers a la ciutat d'Agen: so es a ssaber, que si la meissa ciutat a guerra, que mestiers aia garnizos, lo senher i deu metre garnizo de .xx. cavers garnits del tot, e de .xxx. sirvents armats a caval, e de .x. balesters a caval, li qual devo defen- [f. 25r] -dre e gardar la ciutat e la vila d'Agen avant dicha, e ·ls habitants del meiss loc dints e deforas, tant quant aquela guerra durara, a las proprias despensas del senhor.

[CHAPTER V]

Quintum capitulum.

Si entre alcus homes o femnas de la ciutat o dels borcs d'Agen a questio de deutes, o de covents, aquel qui volra demandar lo deute o ·l covent deu l'autre enquer[r]e ab testimoni de la meissa ciutat o dels borcs d'Agen. E si aquel a cui volra demandar lo presenta dreghs denant [f. 25v] lo cosselh d'Agen, deu l'i prend(r)e e devo estre ambedoas las partidas denant lo meiss cosseilh al primer dia que s'ajuste apres la enquesta facha. E si aquel qui fara la enquesta demanda fermansa ad aquel qui ·l presentara dreghs denant lo cosselh, deu lo fermar si pot per fermansa parlant, o per sagrament si per fermansa parlant no pot, que el lo fasa dreghs a esgart del dighs cosselh. E si no lo fermava aissi cum dessus es dighs, pot s'en clamar al senhor, salb

other men. These porters must take in all the salt in sacks from the ship outside by the Montcorni gate and then the said porters must take it back from here to the banks of the Garonne and discharge it into a ship from Agen that will take it upstream, and not into another ship. But the owner of the salt must make an agreement with the said porters who carry the salt that he will pay them the wages he has negotiated with them. And if a man transported salt up-stream in the hold [*en sola*] of a ship above the said pillars which was not measured and carried from within the said gate as was said above, the salt-lord would get 65 arnaldenc sous as a fine and the salt will be confiscated [*encorsa*]. And if men from Agen took shares [*peciavo*] in that ship, they could do so, and they are not obliged to the lord or to any one else if they took shares. And [f. 24r] no ship may transport salt upstream by the river Lot in any manner. And if someone did, the ship and the salt would be confiscated by the salt-lord of Agen and the salt-lord would get 65 arnaldenc sous as a fine from each man who was transporting the salt upstream. ¶ No man may transport salt using animals or by any other method through Gascony from the bridge of Barbaste[10] upstream, nor from Aiguillon[11] upstream between the Lot and the Garonne[12] unless he obtained it from the Agen salt business. And if anyone does, the salt-lord gets 65 arnaldenc sous as a fine and the salt and the animal that was carrying it are confiscated. But any man living beyond the Garonne who comes to buy salt at the Agen salt business can get the salt he wants, for 12 arnaldenc deniers per *mealha* less than it is sold at the salt business. And the salt-lord must earn [f. 24v] on the salt he sells one-third more money that he has bought it for, and no more than that. Item: No man or woman who retails salt in Agen must mix any but the salt they have bought at the salt store with what they sell in Agen or outside it. And if they did, the salt-lord would get from him or her 65 arnaldenc sous as a fine and the salt {would be} confiscated. And for the above said salt business and for the fractions [*punheras*] and for the measurement {fees} of the afore said wheat the lord must perform the following duties for the city of Agen. That is to say if the said city is at war so that it needs a garrison, the lord must furnish a garrison of 20 completely equipped knights and 30 armed mounted soldiers [*sirvents*] and 10 mounted crossbowmen. They are to defend [f. 25r] and protect the above said city and town of Agen and the residents of the said place inside and out {the walls} as long as the war shall last, and at the lord's personal expense.

[CHAPTER V]

Fifth chapter.

If there is a dispute about debts or agreements between men or women of the city of Agen or its suburbs, the person wishing to lodge the complaint on debt or agreement must seek a settlement [*enquerre*][13] from the other in the presence of a witness from the said city or suburbs of Agen. And if the person from whom he is asking {for the settlement} seeks a trial [*lo presenta dreghs*] before [f. 25v] the Agen council he must accept it there and both parties must appear before the said council on the first day when they sit after the attempt at settlement. And if the person seek– ing settlement requires an assurance [*fermansa*] from the person seeking a trial before the council, {the latter} must give him an assurance, using a personal surety if he can, or by his oath if he cannot obtain a personal surety, that he will carry out the verdict

que en batezo, ni en maldighs, ni en raubaria, ni en mala facha, ni en crim no a enquesta, ans s'en pot hom clamar senes enquesta. E tots hom de la ciutat o dels borcs d'Agen pot se clamar d'ome estranh senes enquesta. E si l'estranh [f. 26r] se clamava d'ome d'Agen senes enquesta, deu lo gitar de la maa del senhor. So es a ssaber de .v. sols d'arnaldencs de gatge. Empero si aquel qui dreghs auria presentat devant lo cosselh no era al dia denant lo cosselh per far e per prendre dreghs a esgart del cosselh, lo demandaires s'en pot clamar senes tota enquesta al senhor la hora que ·l cosselhs sera departits. E si negus hom se clamava d'ome d'Agen que no l'agues enqueregut aissi cum dighs es desobre, deu lo gitar de la ma del senhor. So es a ssaber de .v. sols d'arnaldencs de gatge e deu pagar a l'autra partida sas messios si fachas n'avia covinablas a esgart del senhor e de sa cort tant quant conoisseran per jutgament. E si contrast era de la enquesta o contrast era que hom [f. 26v] disses que no l'avia enqueregut o que el l'avia presentat dreghs denant lo cosselh d'Agen aissi cum predich es, aquel a cui seran jutgat li testimoni deu aver .viii. dias continuables per proar e si ad aquel dia proar no podia, deu mentaure los testimonis en secret al senhor e a sa cort e deu far segrament al senhor e a sa cort que no o fa per defucha; e apres lo senher deu far venir en la cort los testimonis e deu los enquerre ab sa cort e far escriure lors dichs quant li testimoni auran presents las partidas jurat dire vertat d'aquo dont seran trachs testimoni tant be per l'una part cum per l'autra. E la corts deu estre de proshomes d'Agen. [CHAPTER VI][14] E al dia de la resposta quant venra al principal del plaghs devo far ambedoas las partidas sagrament de calompnia [f.27r] aguts los dias costumables. So es a ssaber .viii. dias continuables per cosselh, e .viii. dias continuables per resposta; pero si i avia carta publica, non deu hom aver mas .iii. dias continuables per resposta apres los .viii. dias de cosselh e .viii. dias continuables per razonador, si o requer la partida a cui ops sera. E d'aqui en la, deu lo demandaires demandar per sagrament, e ·l defendaires respondre per sagrament. E si i a neg que aquel a cui hom demandara negue aquo que l'autra partida lo demandara, aquel qui fara la demanda o pot proar si ·s vol e pot ne aver .iii. dias cadau de .viii. dias continuables. Mas pero si defalhia que al primer dia no presentassa en la cort alcu dels testimonis que traghs [f.27v] auria, lo senher auria sobre lui .v. sols d'arnaldencs de gatge, si leials excusatios no l'en defendia. E si li testimoni venir no volio en la cort per aquel qui traghs los auria, e dizia que aver no los podia, lo senher a requesta d'aquel qui traghs los auria, agut sagrament de lui que no o fa per defucha e que fagh som poder per lui venir no volio en la cort: deu ab sa cort aquels testimonis far venir en la cort; e si ops es, deu les destrenher per bonas penhoras que deu prendre de lor

[*fasa dreghs*] as ruled by the said council. And if he did not give the assurance as said above, {the plaintiff} can make his complaint to the lord; except that in battery or defamation or robbery or misdemeanor [*mala facha*] or {serious} crime there is no attempt at settlement, but you can make the complaint without attempting settlement. And any man of the city or suburbs of Agen can lodge a complaint against a foreigner [*ome estranh*] without attempted settlement. And if a foreigner [f. 26r] lodged a complaint against a man from Agen without an attempted settlement, it should be refused by the lord's court. This means a fine of 5 arnaldenc sous. However, if the person seeking a trial before the council was not there before the council on the day to make his case and hear the verdict, as ruled by the council, the plaintiff can make his complaint to the lord, without any attempt at settlement, as soon as the council has adjourned [*departits*]. And if some man lodged a complaint against a man of Agen, and had not attempted settlement as described above, it should be thrown out. That means 5 arnaldenc sous as a fine, and he must pay the other party for his reasonable expenses, if he had any, as ruled by the lord and his court, as much as they rule in a judgment. And if there was a dispute about the offer of settlement, or there was a dispute where a man [f. 26v] said that he had not been asked for a settlement, or that a hearing had been sought before the council of Agen as was said above, then the person who, according to the ruling, had to produce witnesses must have a court date eight days later to make his proof, and if on that day he could not make his proof, he should name the witnesses secretly to the lord and his court, and he must take an oath to his lord and his court that he is not doing so fraudulently, [*per defucha*] and after that the lord must make the witnesses appear in the court and he must question them with his court and have what they say written down, once the witnesses have sworn, in the presence of the parties, to tell the truth concerning what they were called to witness to, for one side as for the other. And the court must be made up of goodmen [*proshomes*] of Agen.

[CHAPTER VI]

And on the response day, when they come to the principal issue of the trial, both parties must swear an oath of calumny [*de calompnia*], [f. 27r] once they have taken the customary delays. That is, 8 days to seek counsel, and 8 days to answer, but if there is a public instrument there should be only 3 days for an answer, after the 8 days for seeking counsel and 8 days to find an advocate [*razonador*] if the party needing one asks for this delay; and from then on the plaintiff must make his request under oath and the defendant answer under oath. And if there is a denial, if the person being sued denies what the other party is asking for, the person making the demand can prove it, if he wishes, and he can have three court dates, at 8 day intervals. But if he defaults, so that on the first court date he does not present to the court any of the witnesses that he has called, [f. 27 v] then the lord gets from him a fine of 5 arnaldenc sous, unless he has a valid [*leial*] excuse in his defense. And if the witnesses would not appear in court for the person calling them, and he said he could not produce them, the lord, at the request of the person calling them, once he had received his oath that he was not acting fraudulently, and that after he had done his best they would not appear on his behalf, {the lord} and his court should have those witnesses brought to the court, and if necessary he should distrain them by means of

per portar testimoni a la vertat d'aquo sobre que seran traghs testimonis. E per meissa manera es dighs del cosselh d'Agen dels plaghs que venran denant lor. E si aquel qui traghs los aura per testimonis dizia que sei testimoni no ero en la vila, o que ero a sanc- [f.28r] -tor, o ero malaute, o en mercadaria, o per cocha de senhor o de la vila, lo senher ab sa cort deu dar dia a lui a esgart del cosselh d'Agen ab sagrament que no o fa per defucha. Pero en questio de raubaria ni de crim no deu hom aver dia, mas que ades senes tots perlongaments responda a son acusador. Salb que si testimonis i a ops, sobre aquo pot aver aquel qui ops los aura a traire tots sos dias costumables aissi cum avant dighs es, la ont parla de la productio dels testimonis.

[CHAPTER VII]

De negu contrast o plaghs que fos entre homes d'Agen, e entre homes defora e homes d'Agen, negus no pot proar contra home d'Agen si testimoni d'Agen no i avia. E si alcus hom d'Agen [f. 28v] avia questio ni contrast ab autrui deforas que o pot proar ab testimonis d'Agen o deforas, si hom als dichs o a las personas d'aquels testimonis no podio dire causa [usa][15] razonabla per que lor testimonis no pogues valer.

[CHAPTER VIII]

Tota demanda que hom fasa a home d'Agen dont lo senher aia clam, e tota demanda que ·l senher fassa a home d'Agen, deu estre plageada e termenada e jutgada a Agen, senes que l'om d'Agen non es tenguts issir plagear en negu loc deforas Agen per lo senhor ni per autrui. Pero si alcus hom privats o estranhs demandava a Agen alcu covent o alcu deute que disses que fos faghs deforas Agen ad al- [f. 29r] -cu home d'Agen, e ·n avia carta leial e publica, pot o proar ab la carta; o si carta non avia, e l'hom d'Agen creia re d'aquel covent o d'aquel deute, l'om defora o pot proar aqui ont lo covents o ·l deutes fo faghs e l'om d'Agen es li tenguts seguir. Mas tots hom d'Agen pot proar tota causa que demande a home estranh ab testimonis d'Agen o defora, qual que mais se vulha ni aver pusca.

[CHAPTER IX]

Si plaghs era a Agen entre homes d'Agen o d'estranhs sobre heretats, o terras, o autras causas que hom demandes per razo de parentat, e neg i avia que ·l parentat no fos creuts, aquel parentats deu estre proats a Agen o defora, ab testimonis d'Agen [f. 29v] o defora, tant quant al gra del parentat aperte, aqui ont melhs aquel qui ops o aura o poira proar; quar en mants locs a hom parents per successio e per escaensa, dels quals aveno mantas drechuras a mants homes, lo qual parentat, si plaghs n'era, a

good security which he should take from them to bear witness to the truth concerning the matter on which they were called as witnesses. And the same is said for the Agen council concerning suits coming before them. And if the person calling the witnesses said that his witnesses were not in the city, or they had gone on a pilgrimage [*a sanctor*] [f. 28r] or were sick, or on a voyage as a merchant [*en mercadaria*] or on the lord's or the city's business, the lord and his court should give him a court date, by the ruling of the council of Agen, on his oath that he was not doing this fraudulently. But in cases of robbery or {serious} crime a man should not get another court date, but must answer his accuser right away without any delays. Except that if witnesses are needed, the person requiring to call them can have all his cus–tomary delays as was said above, where it talks about the production of witnesses.

[CHAPTER VII]

In any dispute or suit between men of Agen, or between men from outside and men of Agen, no one can make proof against a man from Agen unless there is a witness from Agen. And if any man from Agen [f. 28v] had a disagreement [*questio*] or a dispute with someone outside[16] he could make proof with witnesses from Agen, or from outside, unless a reasonable cause can be put forward as to why the testimony of these witness is not valid, because of what they say or who they are.

[CHAPTER VIII]

Any suit brought against a man of Agen of which the lord has jurisdiction, and any suit brought by the lord against a man of Agen must be pleaded and completed and judged in Agen, without the man from Agen being obliged by the lord or any one to go and plead in any place outside Agen. But if any man from within [*priuats*] or outside sued in Agen on any agreement or any debt that he said was made outside Agen by some [f. 29r] man from Agen, and he had a valid and public instrument on the subject, he can make proof with the document; but if he did not have a document, and the man from Agen admitted [*creia*] nothing {something?} about this agreement or this debt, the man from outside can make proof at the place where the agreement or debt was made, and the man from Agen is obliged to follow him there. But any man from Agen can make proof in any suit he lodges against a man from outside with witnesses from Agen or outside, whichever he prefers or can obtain.

[CHAPTER IX]

If there were a suit at Agen between men of Agen or strangers concerning inherited or other land, or other things that a man might petition for because of kinship, and there was a denial, so that the kinship was not accepted as proved [*creuts*]: that kinship must be proved in Agen or outside with witnesses from Agen [f. 29v] or from outside, as many as are required {to prove} the degree of kinship, at the place where the person with the burden of proof can best make his proof; for in many places a person has kinsfolk, through whom, by a succession or a lateral inheritance [*escaensa*], many rights come to many men. If there were a suit about this kinship, it

greu n'en neguna maneira poiria hom proar, si no per los vezis del loc o dels locs dont aquilh parent aurio estat habitador.

[CHAPTER X]

Eras digam dels clams qui veno denant lo senhor en qual manera lo senher o deu far, e cum las principals personas, so es lo demandaires e ·l respondeires, devo lo plaghs perseguir e cum se devo far terra garda e reire garda, e quants dias ne deu hom aver. [f. 30r]

Si lo senher a clam d'ome d'Agen de deute, o de covent, o de forsa, o de perturbacio de terras, o de feus, o de possessios, o d'autra causa que toque a deute, o ad alcu covent, o a dessaziment, deu lo senher auzir ab sa cort, que deu estre de pros–homes d'Agen, tot lo plaghs per tots los dias costumables tro al desfiniment del plaghs. Lo qual plaghs deffinits lo senhor deu aver .v. sols d'arnaldencs de gatge del vencut. Mas avant que aia son gatge, deu ad aquel qui aura son plaghs vencut far complir aquo [f. 30v] que ·l sera conogut per si o per jutjament; e ·l deu far redre sas messios razonablas al esgart del senhor e de sa cort. E si neguna deffalha era demandada de dia assignat a neguna de las partidas del senhor o d'alcuna de las partidas, e la deffalha era creuda o proada de l'autra part per testimonis sufficients si neg i avia, lo senher auria .v. sols d'arnaldencs de gatge d'aquel deffa[l]hit; o si l'autra parts aquela defalha proar no podia, o si ·l senher aquela defalha demandava per si, si aque l a cui aquela defalha seria demandada no auzava jurar sobre ·ls sants evangelis que defalhits no fos, lo senher auria sobre lui .v. sols d'arnaldencs de gatge si per leial excusatio defendre no s'en podia, e l'autra parts [f. 31r] sas messios razonablas a conoguda del senhor e de sa cort. E es a ssaber que de tot plaghs que sia sobre terras, o heretats, o possessios pot aver aquel a cui ops sera .v. dias continuables per terra garda, e .iii. dias continuables per reire garda, si o demanda ni o requer en son loc, auzida la demanda. Mas si aquel qui deura far la terra garda la vol ades far, l'autre li deu ades seguir coras que ·s volha, si o requer, dints los predighs .v. dias, e l'autre ades aqui meiss far a lui la reire garda si se vol, denant cui que aquel plaghs sia. ¶Item: si alcus se clama al senhor d'alcu home d'Agen, e ·l senher lo demanda fermansa, deu lo dar fermansa si pot, o deu passar ab sagrament que fassa que fermar no pot, e que ·l plaghs [f. 31v] persegua a esgart del senhor e de sa cort. Pero si aquel de cui hom se sera clamatz requer que vol veire lo clamant e auzir sa demanda, deu lo clamants venir en la cort e far sa demanda e puis aquel de cui se sera clamats deu fermar lo meiss dia per fermansa o per sagrament, aissi cum predighs es. E si lo meiss dia, aissi cum predighs es, no fermava, lo senher auria sobre lui .v. sols d'arnaldencs de gatge. Mas si lo senher fazia neguna demanda per si meis ad alcu home d'Agen, no l'es tenguts l'om d'Agen fermar mas per sa ma; ni ·l senher no pot proar neguna causa contra negu home d'Agen, si

could scarcely be proved in any way except by the neighbors of the place or places where these kinsfolk had been residents.

[CHAPTER X]

Now we {will} speak of suits that come before the lord, how the lord should proceed, and how the principal persons, that is the plaintiff [*demandaires*] and the defendant [*respondeires*], should prosecute the claim, and how a *terra garda* and a *reire garda*[17] are peformed, and how many court dates a man should be given for them. [f. 30r]

If the lord has {jurisdiction over} a claim [*a clam*] against a man from Agen for debt, or or for an agreement, or on violence, or disturbance of lands or fiefs, or on possession, or for some other reason involving debt, or some agreement, or disseisin, the lord should hear it with his court, which must consist of goodmen of Agen, on all the customary court dates until the suit is ended. Once the suit is ended, the lord should receive 5 arnaldenc sous as a fine from the loser. But before {the lord} collects his fine, he must execute what [f. 30v] is adjudged to the winner of the suit by himself or the court. And {the winner} must have his reasonable expenses reimbursed upon the ruling of the lord and his court. And if a default of an assigned court date was claimed against one of the parties by the lord or one of the parties, and the default was admitted [*creuda*], or proved using adequate [*sufficients*] witnesses by the other side [*de l'autre part*] if it was denied, the lord would receive 5 arnaldenc sous as a fine from the defaulter. But if the other side could not prove the default or if the lord was requesting the default for himself, if the person against whom the default was alleged did not dare swear on the Holy Gospels[18] that he had not defaulted, the lord would receive 5 arnaldenc sous from him if he could not raise the defense of a reasonable excuse. And the other party [f. 31r] {would receive} his reasonable expenses as estimated by the lord and his court. And it should be known that in any suit on land or inherited land, or possession, any one who needs it may have 5 days for an inspection [*terra garda*] and 3 days for a counter-inspection [*reire garda*] if he asks for it or requests it in his turn [*en son loc*] once the complaint has been heard. But if the person who is to show the land wants to do it right away, the other party must follow him whenever he wants if he requests it within the aforesaid 5 days and the other person {can} give the counter-inspection right away to him if he wants, in the presence of [*denant*] whoever has jurisdiction ¶ If[19] some one makes a complaint to the lord about any man from Agen, and the lord asks him for security [*fermansa*] he must give him security if he can or he must give instead an oath he swears that he cannot give security and that he will [f. 31v] prosecute the suit to a ruling by the lord and his court. But if the man about whom a complaint is made wants to see the plaintiff and hear his complaint, the plaintiff must come to court and make his plea [*demanda*], and then the person about whom the complaint is made must give security on the same day by security or an oath, as was said above. And if he did not give security on the same day, as was said above, the lord would receive from him 5 arnaldenc sous as a fine. But if the lord was himself making a demand to some man from Agen, the man from Agen is not required to give security except by his oath {by raising his hand [*per sa ma*]}. And the lord cannot make proof in any suit against any man from Agen, ex-

no o fazia per sa cort bastida que deu estre de pros–homes d'Agen. E tota penhora que ·l senher fassa a home o a femna d'Agen, deu dar lo senher a ma levar ab fermansa. [f.32r] E tot issament tots hom e tota femna pot malevar ab fermansa que presente al defendedor tota causa mobla o no-mobla en que hom o femna lo meta defendement que el o hom o femna per lui aia ni tenga ni que hom o femna lo deia.

[CHAPTER XI]

Cum li cosselh sio establit en las ciutats per goernament d'aquels qui i habito, e sio li cosselh mejancer entre ·ls poderos e ·ls frevols, e entre ·ls rics e ·ls paubres, e a mantener las senhorias dels senhors lors princes, digam cal remedi an el cosseilh d'Agen segont los ancias usatges de la meissa ciutat li habitant del meiss loc, aquil majorment qui en jutjaments se sento gravats. [f. 32v] Quant lo senhor, so es a ssaber sos sen(es)calcs, o sos balles, o alcus jutges aura jutgat a Agen, o en sos apertenements, si neguna de las partidas se tenia per gravada del jutgament, pot sobre aquel grevament apelar al cosselh d'Agen. E si ·l cosselhs conoiss que melhurament i aia ops, aquel jutges i deu melhurar al esgart del meiss cosselh. Pero aquel qui apelara deu fermar ad aquel jutge e a sa cort de perseguir l'apellacio per fermansa o per sagrament, qual que pusca. E si lo cosselhs conois que be aia jutgat, a lo senher o aquel denant cui aquel plagh sera .v. sols d'arnaldencs de gatge sobre aquel qui apelat auria. E si segrament es jutgats a neguna de las partidas sobre diffiniment del plaghs denant lo senhor, [f. 33r] si aquel a cui lo sagraments sera jutgats no l'auza far, lo senher a sobre lui .v. sols d'ardaldencs de gatge de tot plaghs dont lo senher agues agut clam, e l'autra partida auria som plaghs atenhs, e sas messios razonablas al esgart del senhor e de sa cort.

[CHAPTER XII]

Despoiss que de mantas causas bezonhablas avem tractat desobre, tractem cum cadaus se garde cum metra autrui em plaghs si a razo ni dreghs per que ·l deia metre em plaghs, que no ·l tribalhe en va ni no-degudament.

Quar mants homes comenso calonjar e demandar mantas causas per barat, [f.33v] per tribalhar autrui contra cui no an drechurera actio, mas per aver rehemso de lui, o per far lo seu metre per lor maleza, e quant an comensat home trabalhar per semblansa de dreghs aqui ont no an dreghs, se laisso de lor demanda quant an home pro tribalhat, o ·n an rehemso per que se laisso de lui tribalhar, es acostumat per los ancias que si alcus hom o alcuna femna comensa moure a home o a femna a Agen plaghs o questio en cort, denant qualque jutge, e aquel qui aura comensat a demandar

cept by his official court [*cort bastida*] which must consist of goodmen of Agen. And any property that is seized from a man or woman of Agen the lord should release on{the person's} oath with security [*fermansa*]. [f. 32r] And in just the same way any man or woman can, with security to the defendant, obtain release [*malevar*] from someone disputing ownership of any personal property or non-personal property that some man or woman is disputing {his ownership of}, and that he or some man or woman on his behalf may have or hold, or that a man or woman owes him.

[CHAPTER XI]

And since councils are established in cities for the government of those who live there, and the councils are in the middle [*meiancer*] between the powerful and the weak, and between the rich and the poor, and to maintain the lordship of the lords [who are] their rulers [*princes*], we will say what remedies the inhabitants of the said city have in the council of Agen, according to the ancient practices [*ancias usatges*] of the said city, especially those who feel they have been injured[20] by a judgment. [f. 32v]. When the lord, that is to say the seneschal or his *balle*, or some judge has judged in Agen or in its dependencies [*apartenements*] if any of the parties feels injured by the judgment he can appeal concerning that injury to the council of Agen. And if the council agrees that there needs to be some correction [*melhuramen*], that judge must correct it according to the ruling of the said council. But the appellant must confirm [*fermar*] to that judge and his court, by giving security or an oath, whichever he can, that he will prosecute the appeal. And if the council judges that he had judged well, the lord or the person before whom the suit was brought will get 5 arnaldenc sous as a fine from the person who appealed. And if an oath is ruled required of any of the parties concerning the bringing of the suit to a close before the lord, [f. 33r] if the person from whom the oath has been ruled to be required does not dare swear it, the lord gets from him 5 arnaldenc sous as a fine for each suit in which the lord had jurisdiction, and the other party will have won his suit, and will also get his reasonable costs on the ruling of the lord and his court.

[CHAPTER XII]

Now that we have dealt above with many kinds of necessary [*bezonhables*] suits we will deal with how each person should be careful how he sues others in lawsuits, if he has a good reason or a law under which he should sue the other person, so that he does not harass [*tribalhe*] him in vain or improperly [*no-degudament*].

Many men begin to make challenges[21] [*caloniar*] and to lay many claims fraud–ulently[*per barat*], [f. 33v] in order to harass persons against whom they have no rightful claim, but in order to get a pay-off [*rehemso*] from them or to make them spend money [*lo seu metre*] out of malice, and when they have begun to harass a man under color of right where they have no right, they abandon their claim when they have thoroughly harassed a man or received a pay-off, so that they cease harassing them. For this reason it was a custom among the ancients that if some man or woman began to lodge a complaint, or demand something, against a man or woman from Agen, before some judge in a court, and the person who had lodged the complaint

cessava de sa demanda que aura comensada, que no la perseguis, o que el gurpisca al defendedor aquo que l'aura comensat a demandar, o mene lo plaghs tro a diffinicio senes no-deguts alongaments, e ref- [f.34r] -fassa a l'autra part las despessas que fachas aura per aquel plaghs a conoguda del jutge e de sa cort d'aquela causa, si ·l plaghs perseguir no vol. E aquel qui d'aquo sera jutges per son offici lo fassa quitar e solver d'aquela demanda, e l'en fassa dar carta de perpetual quitacio d'aquel qui, aussi cum predighs es, l'aura en va tribalhat, si aquel a cui aura ops o requer e o demanda. E si, aissi cum predighs es, quitar o menar som plaghs e sa demanda no vol amonestats d'aquel qui ·n sera jutges, ni redre no vol a l'autra partida sas despessas taxadas e juradas, pot s'en clamar aquela parts aissi cum predighs tribalhada es al senhor, senes tota enquesta. E ·l senher deu lo constrenher per bonas penhoras qu'en prenga que el gurpisca aquela demanda [f.34v] al Reu, so es a ssaber a aquel a cui demandara, o que mene lo plagh aissi cum deura. E si ·l senher costrenher aissi cum predighs es no l'en volia, lo cosselhs d'Agen l'en deu destrenher a requesta d'aquel a cui ops sera.

[CHAPTER XIII]

Apres conseguentre parlem en qual manera deu hom traire garent, ni quants dias ne pot hom aver segont las costumas d'Agen, e cum aquel qui sera traghs garents o deu far.

Si alcus tra garent en cort d'alcuna causa que hom lo demande, pot ne aver .viii. dias continuables si o requer. E si al meiss dia no a son [f. 35r] garent en cort, deu lo mentaure a la cort, e ab sagrament que fasa que som poder n'a faghs e aver no l'a pogut, e que no o fa per defucha ni per mal genh, pot ne aver .viii. dias continuables, e autres .viii. dias continuables segondament, e autres .viii. dias tersa vets, si o demanda e o requer ab los dighs sagrament que fasa a cada dia. Mas d'aqui en la non deu aver plus dia. Salb aitant que si dizia que sos garents per lui venir no volia, deu s'en clamar al senhor, e ab lo senhor e en totas maneras deu far som poder que venga en la cort per portar la garentia que deura. E endemeghs deu cessar lo plaghs sobre ·l principal, entro que aquel que lo garent deura traire aia faghs som poder de son ga- [f. 35v] -rent aver al bon albire del senhor e de sa cort. Pero si aquel qui lo garent traira di que sos garents es fora la terra, deu lo mentaure en la cort, e deu jurar sobre ·ls sants evangelis que aquel es sos garents, e que no o fa per mal genh, e deu aver dia sobre aital cas per aver son garent a bona estimacio del senhor e de sa cort, segont que conoissera lo senher ab sa cort que aquel garent sera lonh o pres. En dimeghs deu lo plaghs del principal cessar. Pero si ·l garents ve en la cort, cum garents deu fermar, e si fermar no vol o no pot, no val sa garentia, quar no es dreghs garents que sa garentia abondozament no ferma. E si faghs som poder aissi cum predighs es, so es a

abandoned the claim he had instituted, so that he did not prosecute it, then either he must quit-claim [*gurpisca*] to the defendant the thing he had begun to lay claim to, or else he must prosecute the claim to conclusion without any improper dilatoriness, and must [f. 34r] reimburse the other party for the expenses he had had in the suit, at the estimation of the judge and his court for the suit, if he did not want to continue to prosecute. And the person who is the judge of this matter should as part of his duty make {the plaintiff} declare {the defendant} free and clear of this claim, and make the person who had, as said above, harassed him in vain give him a perpetual quit-claim instrument, if the person who needs it requests it or asks for it. And if {the plaintiff}, after being warned by the person who has jurisdiction as judge, will not abandon or prosecute his suit or claim, as described above, nor reimburse the other party his assessed and sworn expenses, then the party who has been harassed as described above can lodge a complaint with the lord without any attempted set–tlement [*enquesta*]. And the lord, by confiscating good security from him, must compel {the harassing party} to abandon this claim [f. 34v] against the defendant [*reu*], that is to say to the person he has been laying the claim against, or else pro–secute the claim as he ought. And if the lord will not compell him as was said, above, the council of Agen should compel him at the request of a person who needed it.

[CHAPTER XIII]

After {this} we continue by saying how a person should vouch a warrantor [*traire garent*] and how many court dates a person can have according to the customs of Agen, and how the person who is vouched as a warrantor should act.

If someone vouches a warrantor[22] in court in some matter where he is being sued, he can have {a continuance of} eight days if he requests it. And if on the given day he does not have his [f. 35r] warrantor in court, he should announce this to the court, along with an oath he should swear that he has done his best, and has not been able to obtain his appearance, and that he is not doing this fraudulently nor im–properly, {whereupon} he can get {a continuance of} 8 days and another {of} 8 days a second time and another {of} 8 days a third time, if he asks for it and requires it with the said oath that he swears on each appearance; but after that he should not get another court date. Except that if he said that his warrantor would not appear on his behalf, he should complain to the lord, and with {the help of} the lord and by all means he should do his best to have him appear in the court and be his warrantor as he should; and meanwhile the suit on the substance should stop until the person who is to vouch the warrantor has done his best to have the warrantor [f. 35v] appear, to satisfaction of the lord and his court. But if the person vouching the warrantor says his warrantor is out of the district, he should state this to the court, and swear on the Holy Gospels that the person is his warrantor, and that he is not claiming this im–properly; and he should have a court date to obtain his warrantor at the best estimate of the lord and his court, according to what the lord and his court know about how far away or how near the warrantor is; meanwhile the suit on the substance should stop. But if the warrantor appears in the court, then as a warrantor he should give se–curity, and if he will not or cannot give security, his warranting is not valid; for he is no true warrantor who does not give abundant security. And if the person vouching

ssaber qu'en agues aguts tots sos dias a conogu- [f. 36r] -da del senhor e de sa cort, e si ·l garents no fermava aissi cum predighs es, d'aqui en la no pot aver garent en aquel plaghs, ans deu anar avant el plaghs per si meiss ab son aversari tant quant deura. E tots garents, quant fermat aura, deu aver .viii. dias continuables per resposta tant solament, senes que no deu aver plus dia per cosselh ni per als mas que al meiss dia responga cum garents aissi cum deura.

[CHAPTER XIV]

Per so quar li pes e las liuras e autras mezuras devo estre leials, quar per aquo son establidas en las ciutats, que ni ·l vendeires ni ·l compraires no ·i sia enganats, parlem de las mezuras d'oli, e de las liuras, e dels marcs, e de las pezas [f. 36v] e de las canas ab que hom cana los draps, dont hom uze en vendent et en comprant, si no ero leials qu'en deu estre faghs.

Si negus hom o neguna femna tenia a Agen mezura d'oli que no fos leials ab la qual mezura[s] o ·n agues mezurat vendent e comprant, lo senher i auria .lxv. sols d'arnaldencs de gatge, e la mezura seria peciada. E la liura ab que hom peza o mezura deu estre de .xvi. onsas. E si negus hom o neguna femna avia liura a Agen que no fos leials, qu'en vendes ni ·n compres, lo senher i auria .lxv. sols d'arnaldencs de gatge, e la liura seria peciada. E ·l marcs [f. 37r] ab que hom peza deu estre drechurers al marc de Colonha, e deu estre de .xvi. onsas. E si negus hom o neguna femna avia autre marc que no fos leials, aissi cum predighs es, ab lo qual hom pezes en vendent o en comprant, lo senher i auria .lxv. sols d'arnaldencs de gatge, e ·l marcs seria peciats. E si las pezas ab que hom peza si hom ne trobava sobre alcu, ab las quals vendes e compres, o ·n agues vendut o comprat, que no fosso leials ni drechureiras, lo senher i auria .lxv. sols d'arnaldencs de gatge e las pezas serio peciadas. E las canas ab que hom cana los draps devo estre leials cadauna de .viii. palms comunals. E si negus hom o neguna femna canava ab cana que no fos leials en vendent o en comprant, lo senher [f. 37v] i auria .lxv. sols d'arnaldencs de gatge, e la cana seria peciada. E deu lo senher conoisser ab lo cosselh d'Agen de las mezuras, e de las liuras, e dels marcs, e de las pezas, e de las canas si son leials o no, avant que ·l senher re n'aia.

[CHAPTER XV]

Justicia, so es drechura, e es comandada de Deu que sia gardada en terra. E quar pluzors homes e femnas dario tot lor entendement a mal far si li mal per justicia, so es per drechura, no ero refrenat, es aitals justicia a Agen ancianament aprobada, que de tot home e de tota femna que fara laironeci de noghs son las suas causas encorsadas al senhor, la causa panada restaurada ad aquela persona a cui lo laironicis sera faghs, si

the warrantor has done his best as was said above, that is to say that he has taken all his delays [f. 36r] to the knowledge of the lord and his court, and also if the warrantor did not give security [*fermaua*] as was said above, from then on {the defendant} cannot have a warrantor in that suit, but he must proceed alone with the suit against his opponent, as long as it lasts. And any warrantor when he has given security should have {a continuance of} eight days to prepare his response and that is all, without getting another delay [*dia*] to obtain counsel or for anything else; but on the said day he should respond as a warrantor, as he should.

[CHAPTER XIV]

Because the weights and the *liure*[23] and other measures must be exact [*leials*],[24] since they are established in cities so that neither the seller nor the buyer will be cheated, let us speak of measures for oil, and *liures* and marks, and weights [f. 36v] and the cloth-measures [*canas*] used to measure cloth, which are used in selling and buying, {and} what should be done if they are not exact.

If any man or any woman in Agen had {possessed} an oil measure that was false, with which they were measuring or had measured in selling or buying, the lord would get 65 arnaldenc sous as a fine, and the measure would be broken; and the *liura* {pound} used to weigh or measure must be 16 ounces [*onsas*]. And if any man or woman had a pound weight [*livre*] in Agen that was not exact, and was using it to buy and sell, the lord would get a fine of 65 arnaldenc sous, and the pound would be broken. And the mark [f. 37r] with which measurements are made must conform to the Cologne mark, and it must be 16 ounces. And if any man or woman of Agen had a different mark, that was not exact, as was said above, which was used for weighing in selling or buying, the lord would get 65 arnaldenc sous as a fine and the mark would be broken. And also the measures use to measure, if one was found on any person with which he or she was buying or selling, or had been buying or selling, and it was false or not conforming [*drechureiras*], the lord would get 65 arnaldenc sous as a fine and the weights would be broken. And the cloth-measures [*canas*] use to measure cloth must each be an honest eight common spans [*palms*]. And if any man or woman was measuring cloth with a measure that was not exact, when selling or buying, the lord [f. 37 v] would get 65 arnaldenc sous as a fine and the cloth-measure would be broken. And the lord should judge [*conoisser*] with the council of Agen concerning measures and pounds and marks and weights and cloth-measures, concerning measures and pounds and marks and weights and cloth measures, concerning whether they are exact or not, before the lord gets any thing {as a fine}.

[CHAPTER XV]

Justice is rightfulness [*drechura*][25] and it is God's command that it be preserved on earth. And because certain men and women would give all their efforts [*entendement*] to doing evil if evil was not controlled [*refrenat*] by justice, that is by right, this justice has been approved of old in Agen: that any man or woman committing larceny by night forfeits to the lord his {or her} personal property [*las suas causas*]; the stolen article is given back to the person from whom it was stolen, if it is found; and

hom la troba, e si no la troba, [f. 38r] deu cobrar lo valent per leial estimacio de las causas del lairo si hom l'en troba, conogut e proat lo laironeci. E si ·l laironecis es de .xx. sols en sus, lo senher deu far de son cors justicia, e si era de .xx. sols en jos, deu estre senhats, pero si hom l'atrobava senhat, lo senher deu far de son cors justicia, pero pagat a sa molher, si ·n a, aquo que ·l deura per son dot o per als, e sos deutes pagats primerament, e avant que ·l senher aia ni prenga re de sa causas. E qui faria laironici de dias, sas causas devo estre encorssas al senhor, pagats sos deutes, e a sa mo(l)her son aver, si molher a, e ·l laires o la laira deu estre senhats o senhada. E si avia senhal, lo senher deu far del cors justicia, salb per causa menjadoira que valgues .xii. deniers o d'aqui [f. 38v] en jos. E si alcus hom o femna metia foc em maio, o em blat, o en fe, o versava, o afolava l'autrui vi, o l'autrui oli, o l'autrui mel, o aucizia l'autrui caval, o l'autrui bestia, o talava l'autrui vinha, o ·ls autrui arbres, o l'autrui blat, passaria pena a esgart del senhor e del cosselh d'Agen, segont que la mala facha seria grans o pauca, e segont que seria facha de dias o de noghs, facha esmenda plenera ad aquela persona que lo dampnatge auria sostengut a esgart del senhor e del cosselh d'Agen. E si hom o femna panava vendenha de l'autrui vinha ab sacs, o ab paners, o ab comportas, o l'autrui blat, o l'autrui fe, o ortalizia d'autrui cazal de noghs, o lenha, o paissel, o coudra, o fusta, lo senher [f. 39r] n'auria .lxv. sols d'arnaldencs de gatge, la causa proada aissi cum deu, facha primerament esmenda ad aquel qui ·l dampnatge auria receubut, a esgart del senhor e de sa cort, la qual corts deu estre del cosselh e dels proshomes d'Agen.

[CHAPTER XVI]

Cum sobre totas las malas fachas que hom fa en terra sio murtres plus venjadors, digam qui plagaria autrui, o qui faria murtre, so es homicidi, qu'en deu estre faghs.

Si lo senher a clam d'alcu home o d'alcuna femna que aia plagat autre ab cotel, o ab ferrament, o ab peira, o ab basto, e sancs n'issia, o l'avia membre fraghs, [f. 39v] a lo senher sobre lui .lxv. sols d'arnaldencs de gatge, la causa proada per sufficiens testimonis, e facha primerament dressa deguda ad aquel qui lo dampnatge auria sustengut, a esgart del senhor e de sa cort. Pero la plaga no deu estre jutgada entrou que sia vist si ·l plagats viura o murra. E si ·l plagats mor d'aquela plaga, totas las causas d'aquel homicidi son encorsas al senhor, pagat aquo que deuria a sa molher e ad autrui tot primerament, e avant que ·l senher agues ni preses sas causas. E del cors d'aquel homici deu lo senher far justicia. So es a ssaber que ·l deu far sotsterrar viu sots lo mort, e aisso deu jutgar lo senher ab sa cort, que deu estre lo cosselhs e li proshome d'Agen. Mas pero si pecs [f. 40r] i avenia en trep saubut per sobreportament de caval, o per encontre, o que hom corregues caval o roci per carreira, o que hom lances peira, o basto, o autra causa a ca o a porc, o jogava hom a

if it is not found [f. 38r], then he {or she} should get back the value, honestly estimated, from the personal property of the thief (if he has any), once the theft has been judged [*conogut*] and proved. And if the theft is of 20 sous or more, the lord should execute him [*far de son cors iusticia*]; and if it was less than 20 sous, he should be branded [*senhats*]; but if he was already found to be branded, the lord should execute him, but his wife if he has one should be paid what he owes her as her dowry or anything else, and his debts should be paid first, and before the lord collects or takes any of his property. And if someone commits a theft by day, his property is forfeit to the lord once his debts are paid, and her property given to his wife if he has one; and a man or woman thief must be branded. And a person already branded should be executed, except for a minor thing worth 12 deniers [f. 38v] or less. And if some man or woman set fire to a house, or to wheat or hay, or spilled or contaminated someone else's wine or oil or honey, or killed someone's horse or other animal, or cut down someone's vines or trees or wheat, he would get a penalty at the ruling of the lord and the council of Agen, according as the misdeed was greater or lesser, and according to whether it was committed by day or by night, once the person sustaining the damage had re–ceived full restitution at the ruling of the lord and the council of Agen. And if a man or woman stole [*panaua*] grapes from someone's vineyard using sacks or baskets or grape-baskets, or someone's wheat or hay, or {took} garden produce from some–one's garden plot by night, or firewood or vine-stakes or coop-rings or timber, the lord [f.39r] would get 65 arnaldenc sous as a fine, once the deed had been proved as it should, once restitution had been made to the person who had suffered the damage, at the ruling of the lord and his court, which court must be {formed} from the council and goodmen of Agen.

[CHAPTER XVI]

Since murders are the most punishable of all the evil deeds that man does on earth, we {will} say what should be done if a person wounds another or commits a murder, that is, homicide.

If the lord receives a complaint about some man or woman alleging he has wounded someone with a knife, or an iron tool or a rock or a stick and it bled, or has broken someone's limb, [f. 39v] the lord gets from him 65 arnaldenc sous as a fine, once thematter is proved by adequate witnesses, and once proper reparations are made to the person who has sustained the damage, at the ruling of the lord and his court; but a judgment should not be issued on a wounding until it has been seen if the injured person will live or die. And if the wounded person dies of the wound, allthe personal property of the homicide are forfeit to the lord, once what he owes has been paid to his wife, and first of all {what he owes} to others, and before the lord may have or take his property; and the lord should execute the homicide. That is to say, that he should have him buried alive under the dead man, and this is what the lord and his court should judge, and the court should be of the council and the goodmen of Agen. But if an accident [*pecs*] [f. 40r] occurred in an acknowledged contest [*trep saubut*] because a horse was out of control [*sobreportament*] or in a collision [*encontre*] or because a man was whipping a horse or pack animal on the street, or a man was throwing astone or a stick or something else at a dog or a pig, or a man was playing at

pressal o a versalh, ab pressa, o ab arc, o ab dart, o si autre pecs i avenia, cum per son cors defendent, o en autra manera, aquel sobre cui aquel pecs seria venguts esmendaria la mala facha e passaria pena, si passar l'en devia, segont la manera del faghs, a conoguda del cosselh e dels proshomes d'Agen.

[CHAPTER XVII]

Mantas vegadas aveno cas sobre murtres e laironecis e autras malas fachas que hom fa en rebost, o en autras mantas maneras que a greu o en neguna manera [f. 40v] poiria estre proat, si no per enquezicio, digam de inquizitio cum ni per quals personas se deu far sobre aitals cas.

Lo senher, o sos senescalx, o sos balles, e ·l cosselhs d'Agen podo far comunal–ment e essemps inquisicio sobre murtres, e sobre laironicis, e sobre autras malafachas, mas lo senher no pot far inquizicio sobre home ni femna d'Agen senes lo cosselh del meiss loc, ni ·l cosseilhs senes lo senhor, o son senescalc, o son balle. Salb pero que si lo senher, o sos senescalcs, o sos balles la enquizicio far no [f. 41r] volia, aissi cum predigs es, lo cosselh d'Agen la deu e la pot far per si meiss, e facha la inquizicio lo senher deu far justicia d'aquel o d'aquela qui del faghs sera covencuts o covencuda, segont que ·l faghs sera o murtres, o laironicis, o autra malafacha. Mas en–pero si alcus hom d'Agen enfranhia pats en autra manera que no toque a murtre, ni a laironici, ni a homicidi, ni a plaga, ni a neguna de las malas fachas avant dichas, deu dar .v. sols d'arnaldencs de gatge al senhor si ·n a clam, e deu esmendar la mala facha d'aquel a cui facha l'aura, a esgart del senhor e del cosselh d'Agen, quant proat sera per abundos testimonis.

[CHAPTER XVIII]

Enaissi cum lo senher principals a sos dreghs [f. 41v] per razo dels dichs encorrements sobre aquela persona sobre cui alcus dels predighs cas o autre, dont las suas causas deguesso estre encorregudas al senhor, avenria, digam si l'encorreguts te a feus re d'autrui, lo senher principals cum ne deu far, e quals costuma n'es sobr'aiso.

Cum en mantas maneras veno encorrements al princi per forfaghs de las gents, es acostumat ancianament a Agen en aital manera, que si encorrements avenia al senhor per alcu forfaghs o en alcuna manera sobre alcu ciutada, o borzes, o habitant d'Agen, e aquel te alcuna [f. 42r] honor, o feus, o heretat, d'alcu home d'Agen a feus, sia clercs sia laics, lo senhor del feus, lo senher, so es lo princis, deu aver venduda, o en autra manera gurpida, aquela causa a feuzater laic qui ·n fasa al senhor d'aquel feus sos devers, lo quals feuzater no sia cavaers, ni clercs, ni d'orde ni de religio, dints un an e un mes que aquel encorrements sera venguts a sa ma. E si dints lo meiss terme

throwing the pallet [*presal*] or target practice [*versalh*] with a pallet, or a bow or a javelin or if some other accident happened, as in self defense or some other way; a person who had been the cause of such an accident would make good the loss [*mala facha*] and suffer a penalty if he had to according the manner of the action, at the estimate of the council and the goodmen of Agen.[26]

[CHAPTER XVII]

Many times cases come on of murder and theft and other offenses that men commit in secret or in many other ways, which can be proved only with difficulty, or not at all [f. 40v] except by an inquiry (*inquizicio*). We will speak of the inquiry, how it can be carried out, and by whom, in such cases.

The lord or his seneschal or his *balle* and the council of Agen can carry out together and as a group an inquiry on murder, or theft or other offenses, but the lord cannot carry out an inquiry on a man or woman of Agen without the council of the said place. Nor [can] the council without the lord or his seneschal or his *balle*. Except, however, that if the lord or his seneschal or his *balle* would not [f. 41r] make an inquiry as said above, then the council of Agen can and should make one by itself; and once the inquiry is over, the lord must punish [*far iusticia de*] the man or woman convicted of the perpetration, according to whether it was murder or theft or some other offense. However if some man from Agen broke the peace in some way that did not involve murder or theft or homicide or a wounding, nor any of the offenses mentioned above, he must give 5 arnaldenc sous to the lord as a fine if he has jurisdiction [*a clam*], and must make restitution to the person on whom he committed {the offense}, at the ruling of the lord and the council of Agen, when it has been proved by sufficient [*abundos*] witnesses.

[CHAPTER XVIII]

Just as the sovereign [*principals*] lord has his rights [f. 41v] by reason of the said seizures from the person concerning whom one of the above cases arose (or others because of which his property [*las suas*] had to be seized by the lord): {now} we {will} speak of what the sovereign lord should do if the person whose property was seized holds some property in fief from some other person; and {we will say} what the custom is in this {situation}.

Since seizures come to the prince in many ways because of people's offenses, the custom in Agen from of old is this way: that if a seizure comes to the lord because of some offense, or in some {other} way, from some citizen or bourgeois[27] or resident of Agen, and the latter holds some [f. 42r] real property [*honor*] or fief or inheritable land from some man of Agen as a fief, whether the lord of the fief was an ecclesiastic or a layman, then the lord, that is the prince, should, within a year and a month of the seizure having come into his hands, have sold or otherwise alienated this property to a secular fiefholder, who can do his duty to the lord of that fief. This fiefholder may not be a knight or an ecclesiastic, nor in orders nor a member of a religious house. And if within the said term {the sovereign} had not installed a fief-

aital feuzater cum predighs es mes no·i avia, d'aqui en la lo senher del feus pot prendre aquel feus per sa propria auctoritat, e tener, e possedir, e uzar, e esplethar tant longament entro que·l senher, so es a ssaber lo princis, i aia mes aital feuzater cum sobredighs es, lo qual aia liurat al senhor d'aquel feus per feuzater. [f. 42v] E per meissa manera es dighs de tota terra o de tota heretat que per testament, o per orde, o per laissa, o per donatio, o en autra manera que sia tenguda o mova a feus d'alcu ciutada o borzes d'Agen avenga per enant, o d'aci en reire sia avenguda, a cavoer, o a clerc, o a maio d'orde, o de religio, o de tota causa, sia {si a?} ordener, o exequtor, o autri aministrador de testaments, o d'orfanhols sio curators, o tutors, o autri aministrador, qui devo aministrar las causas dels morts, tengo ni aministro; pero que sia terra, o maios, o vinha, o autra possessios que sia tenguda a feus d'alcu senhor de feus a Agen e en sos apertenements.

[CHAPTER XIX]

D'ome e de femna pres en adulteri es aitals costu- [f. 43r] -ma a Agen, so es a ssaber que devo corre la vila nu, ligat ambedui d'una corda. E·l senher deu aver .v. sol d'ar–naldencs de gatge sobre cadau. E quant seran espiat, deu lo balles venir al cosselh, o cossels al balle, qualsque primers o sapia. E deu i anar lo balles ab dos proshomes del cosselh o d'aqui en sus, e no senes homes del cosselh que sio dui o plus. E devo estre pres aquil adoltre si son trobat essemps l'us sobre l'autre, e si son nu e nu en un leghs, e que l'om aia las bragas trachas, e no en autra manera. E si l'om pot escapar avant que sia pres, o apres, es quitis, senes que·l senher no·i a re, ne aquel hom non deu passar neguna pena. [f. 43v]

[CHAPTER XX]

No es causa razonabla que negus hom s'enclava de noghs en maio d'autrui, quar majorment es presumptios que per mal far si enclauses que no per be. Ni eissament es de razo que negus intre de dias en la maio d'autrui, quant defendut lo aia. E per esquivar mants murtres, e mants laironecis, o mants autres laghs faghs que s'en poirio enseguir, es tals costuma a Agen sobre aitals cas, so es a ssaber que si alcus ciutadas o borzes d'Agen troba home de noghs enclaus en sa maio, despoiss que sei vezi [f. 44r] seran colcat, deu el e sa molher e sa mainada autaments cridar: "A lairos!" aissi que li vezi o devo be auzir, e deu lo prendre si pot senes plagar e senes aucirre. E si prendre no se laissa, e sobre aquo lui defendent lo senher de la maio, o hom o femna dels seus o per lui, lo plaga o l'auci, non es tenguts el, ne sa molher, ni sa mainada, ni hom ni femna que i sia estats, a senhor ni a vila, ni ad autrui, ab que lo senher de l'ostal, si i es, o sa molher, o sa mainada, si·l senher no·i es, auzo jurar sobre sants evangelis

holder as stated above, then from then on the lord of the fief can by his own au–thority take and hold and exploit {the fief} until the lord, that is to say the prince has installed a fiefholder such as the one described above, whom he has given as a fief–holder to the lord of that fief. [f. 42v] And the same is said of any land, or inheritable land, which, as a result of a testament, or a will or an inheritance or a gift, or in some other way, may be held as a fief or subfief [*moua*] from any citizen or bourgeois of Agen, whether in the past or the future, whether it comes to a knight or an ecclesiastic, or to the house of an order, or a religious house; or {the same is said} of any property, whether a judge [*ordener*][28] or an executor, or some other administrator of wills, or of orphans (whether he is a curator or a tutor), or some other administrators who are supposed to administer the property of the deceased, are holding or admin–istering {it} (provided it is land or houses or vines or some other possession that is held as a fief from some lord of the fief in Agen and its outlying places [*aper–tenements*]).[29]

[CHAPTER XIX]

Concerning a man or woman taken in adultery, this is the custom [f. 43r] in Agen. That is to say that they must run through the town naked tied both with the same cord. And the lord must get 5 arnaldenc sous as a fine from each one. And when they have been detected [*espiat*] the *balle* must come to the council, or the coun-cil must go the *balle*, whoever hears about it first. And the *balle* must go there with two goodmen of the council, or more, and not without two or more men from the council. And the council must go the *balle*, whoever hears about it first. And the *balle* must go there with two goodmen of the council, or more, and not without two or more men from the council. And the adulterers must be arrested if they are found together, one on top of the other, and if they are naked in a bed, and the man has his trousers down [*las bragas trachas*], and in no other manner. And if the man can escape before he is arrested, or after, he is acquitted [*quitis*] without the lord getting anything {as a fine}, and the man should not be subject to any penalty. [f. 43v]

[
CHAPTER XX}

It is not reasonable for any man to be closed up in someone else's house at night, for the greater presumption is that he closed himself up in there to do evil and not to do good. Nor is it reasonable that anyone should enter by day someone else's house when he has been forbidden entry. And to avoid many murders and many thefts, or many other evil deeds [*laghs faghs*] that could ensue, this is the custom in Agen concerning such cases. That is to say that if any citizen or bourgeois of Agen found a man shut up in his house by night, after his neighbors [f. 44r] have gone to bed, he and his wife and his household must cry aloud "Thieves" so that the neighbors are bound to hear. And they must capture him if they can, without wounding him or killing him. And if he will not let himself be captured, and thereupon, while {the intruder} is defending himself the lord of the house or his man or woman, or on his behalf wounds or kills him, neither he nor his wife nor his household, nor any man or woman who was there, is held responsible to the lord or the town or anyone else, provided that the lord of the house, if he was there, or

que no l'aio plagat o mort per autra causa mas quar no se laissava prendre, e que entendio, e creio que per mal far fos intrat en la maio. ¶ Item: si alcus ciutadas o borzes d'Agen avia suspessonos {*sic*} home o femna, [f. 44v] per que ·l defendes sa maio que no ·i intres, e i intrava sobre son defendement, quant lo auria defendut denant dos ciutadas o borzes d'Agen, o d'aqui en sus, e li aontia el o hom o femna, cum de batre o de ferir senes aucire, e senes greument plagar, si es de dias, lo senher de la maio, ni hom ni femna de sa maio, ni qui i sia estats, non son tengut a senhor ni a vila, ni a home ni a femna; pero si de noghs l'i trobava, d'aquo passaria aissi cum dighs es desobre d'ome, si hom lo trobava enclaus de noghs en sa maio. [f. 45r]

[CHAPTER XXI]

Enapres parlem de testimonis fals, qual pena devo passar per castiament d'autres, so es a ssaber que tots hom proats e vencuts per jutgament, o per [propria cofessio, de testimoni que aia portat fals en cort, deu corre la vila ab la lenga traucada ab broca de ferr, e sas causas son encorssas al senhor, pagat primerament aquo que deura a ssa molher e ad autrui, e salb que si te a feus re d'autrui, lo senher deu aver balhat feuzater laic al senhor d'aquel feus dints un an e un mes, aissi cum sober los encorrements es desobre pauzat. E aitals hom fals a pergut {*sic*} per tots temps vots de testimoni e de tota creenssa, so es a ssaber que no pot mais testimoni portar de negu fach, ni lui negus hom creire no deu. [f. 45v]

CHAPTER XXII]

Tots ciutadas e tots borzes d'Agen pot dezamparar sa molher, o son filh, o home o femna que tenga en sa maio, ni a sa soudada, e son home, e son sers, de tot forfaghs que faghs agues, senes que despoiss que l'auria dezemparat, el ni sas causas no son tengut de re al senhor ni ad autrui, si pero no l'enparava. E si hom o femna se clamava al senhor de molher, o de fil, o de sirvent, o de sirventa d'alcu ciutada, o borzes d'Agen, aquel ciutada o borzes no enqueregut, aquel qui [f. 46r] clamats s'en seria lo deu getar de la ma del senhor, tant quant dreghs ne volra far denant lo cosselh d'Agen. Ni si alcus ciutadas o borzes d'Agen batia home o femna de sa mainada, o si sirvent, o sirventa que agues destrenhia per causa que agues preguda en sa maio, o per autra malafacha dont agues sa mainada sospessonoza, pot o far per sa propria auctoritat, senes que non es tengut a senhor ni ad autrui.

his wife or his household if the lord was not there, dare to swear on the Holy Gospels that they did not wound or kill him for any reason except that he would not let himself be captured, and that they understood and believed that he had entered the house with the intention of doing evil. ¶ If any citizen or bourgeois of Agen was suspicious of a man or woman [f. 44v] so that he forbade him to enter his house, and he entered against his order, when it had been given before two or more citizens or bourgeois of Agen, and {the householder}, or some man or woman, shamed him[30] such as by beating or striking him without killing or seriously wounding him, then if it was by day the lord of the house and a man or woman of his house or who was there is not held responsible to the lord or to the city nor to any man or woman; but if he found him by night, he would be treated as was said above about a man if he was found closed up in {someone's} house by night. [f. 45r]

[CHAPTER XXI}

And afterwards let us speak of false witnesses, what punishment they should undergo for the deterrence of others, that is to say that any man proved and condemned [*uencuts*] in court by a judgment, or by his own confession of having given false witness in court must run through the town with his tongue stuck through [*traucada*] with an iron skewer [*broca*]. And his property is forfeited to the lord, once what he owes to his wife and others has been paid; and except that if he holds anything in fief from another, the {sovereign} lord must have provided a secular fief-holder to the lord of that fief within a year and a month, as is laid down [*pauzat*] above on seizures. And such a false man has forever lost the power to testify and to be believed in anything, that is to say that he can no longer give testimony on any action, nor should any man believe him. [f. 45v]

[CHAPTER XXII]

Any citizen and any bourgeois of Agen can repudiate [*dezamparar*] his wife or his son or a man or woman he has in his household in his pay, and his man, and his serf [*sers*] for any offence he has committed, without his or any of his property being liable to the lord or any other person, once he has repudiated them; provided, however, he had not taken them under his protection [*enparava*]. And if a man or woman complained to the lord about a citizen or bourgeois of Agen concerning his wife or his son or his man or woman servant without first attempting a reconciliation [*no enqueregut*], then he [f. 46r] {the person complained about} should get {the matter} out of the lord's court as long as {the complainant} will not appear at a hearing [*drech far*] before the council of Agen. And if any citizen or bourgeois of Agen beat a man or woman of his household, or if he punished a man or woman servant of his for something they had taken from his house, or for some other misdeed for which he suspected {those of} his household: he can do this by his own authority, without being held accountable to the lord or anyone else.

[CHAPTER XXIII]

Eras digam d'ome que deia deute e se reclama per no poder qu'en deu estre faghs. [f. 46v]

Si alcus hom d'Agen deu deute ad autrui, e creut o proat lo deute se reclama per no poder, que diga que no a causa mobla de que pusca pagar lo deute, deu jurar sobre ·ls sants evangelis si ·l creeires, so es aquel a cui deura lo deute, o requer, que no a causa mobla al valent de .v. sols d'arnaldencs ni d'aqui en sus, que pusca pagar a son creedor, e quant poira e aura de que lo pagara aissi cum o gaanhara. E d'aquo pot gitar la messio de si e de sa mainada, de manjar e de beure, e son leghs, e sa archa, e sos garniments, e sos ferraments ab que gaanhara son pa. E cada mes deu far semblant sagrament si l'autre o requer. Pero si lo creeires podia trobar causa mobla que ·l deutres agues, o hom o fem- [f. 47r] -na per lui, que valgues .v. sols o d'aqui en sus, salb las causas desobre exceptadas, lo senher o ·l cosselhs d'Agen lo deu balhar. E si lo deutres demandava dia per terra vendre, que disses que no agues causa mobla dont pogues pagar son deute, aissi cum sobre dighs es, deu aver, fagh sagrament sobre ·ls sants evangelis que no a causa mobla dont pusca pagar, .xl. dias per terra vendre, quant aura mentagut en la cort cal terra vol vendre. E si a la fi de .xl. dias no avia pagat lo deute de venda que agues facha, o en autra manera, lo cosselh d'Agen, a requesta del creedor, lo cosselh d'Agen, a requesta del creedor, deu per son offici d'aqui en la, vendre aquela terra, o aquela honor, facha crida generalment per la vila d'Agen .iii. vegadas [f. 47v] per .iii. dias continuables que aital terra e aital honor volhon vendre, e aquel qui mais i dara aquel l'aura. E deu pagar lo meiss cosselhs d'aquela venda al creedor tant quant poira abastar. E si abastar no ·i podia, lo deutres es tenguts tota hora del remanent, aissi cum o gaanhara e totas las suas causas; e si mais n'avia hom que ·l deutes no montaria, lo mais lo deu hom redre al deutor, pero desfaghs al creedor lo greuh que faghs n'auria, e sas despessas razonablas a bona fe. E ·l creeires pot l'en costrenher ab lo senhor e ab lo cosselh si hom lo troba causa mobla o no-mobla dont lo pusca pagar, salb las causas sobre exceptadas, si de la venda sobre dicha no ·l podia estre pagats sos deutes. [f. 48r]

[CHAPTER XXIV]

Despoissas que avem parlat d'ome qui se reclama per no poder, so es que no pusca pagar lo deute que deu a son creedor de causa mobla que aia, cove que digam d'ome qui empenha maio o autra heretat a son creedor en ma de senhor de feus, dont l'aia dat poder de vendre o d'empenhar, qu'en deu estre faghs, si amonestat de son creedor autrejar no o vol.

[CHAPTER XXIII]

Now let us say what should be done about a man who owes a debt and claims to be unable {to pay}. [f. 46v]

If some man from Agen owes another person a debt, and once the debt is acknowledged or proved, he claims to be unable [to pay], saying that he has no personal property with which to pay the debt, he must swear on the Holy Gospels (if the creditor, that is, the person to whom he owes the debt, wants him to), that he has no personal property to the value of 5 arnaldenc sous or above that he can pay to his creditor, and that when he can, and has the wherewithal, he will pay him as he earns it. And in this way he can exclude enough for himself and his household to eat and drink, and his bed, and his chest, and his clothes [*garniments*] and his iron tools [*ferraments*] with which he can earn his bread. And he must make a similar oath every month if the other party requires it. But if the creditor could find any personal property that the debtor had, or a man or woman [f. 47r] had on his behalf, that was worth 5 sous or more, except the things excluded above, the lord or the council of Agen should give it to him {to the creditor}. And if the debtor asked for a delay [*dia*] to sell some land, saying that he did not have any personal property with which to pay his debt, as said above, then once he had made his oath on the Holy Gospels that he did not have any personal property to pay with, he should get 40 days to sell his land when he has informed the court which land he intends to sell. And if at the end of 40 days he had not paid the debt from the sale he made, or in some other manner, the council of Agen at the re–quest of the creditor should henceforth sell the land or the real property [*honor*] on its own authority, once the public announcement [*crida*] has been generally made in the town of Agen on three occasions, [f. 47v] on three con–secutive days that they want to sell such-and-such a piece of land and such-and such real property [*honor*], and whoever will give most for it shall have it. And from the sale, the said council must satisfy [*abastar*] the creditor as much as it can. And if it cannot satisfy him, the debtor is still held liable for ever [*tota hora*] for the remainder, as he earns {the money} and as to all his property. And if there were more {from the sale} than the debt amounted to, the remainder should be given to the debtor, but with the creditor reimbursed for the trouble he caused him, and for his reasonable expenses in good faith. And the creditor can force him {to pay} with {the help of} the lord if he is found to have some personal property or real property (with the exception of the above mentioned property) with which he might pay him {the creditor}, if he could not be paid what was owed him from the above mentioned sale. [f. 48r]

[CHAPTER XXIV]

Since we have spoken of a man who claims to be unable to pay, that is who cannot pay the debt he owes his creditor out of the personal property he owns, it is right that we should speak of what should be done {when} a man gives to his creditor as security [*empenha*] a house or other real property, in the safekeeping of the lord of the fief, which he has given him power to sell or to give as security [*empenhar*], if he will not hand it over when he is warned by his creditor.

Cum mants homes devo deutes dont cove que enpenha maios, o terras, o autre honor en ma de senhor de feus, es aissi acostumat [f. 48v] per lonc e ancia uzage a Agen, que si alcus deu deute ad autrui dont l'aia enpenhada maio, o terra, o autra honor en ma del senhor d'aquel feus, e l'en aia dat poder de vendre o d'enpenhar, del terme establit de pagar lo deute en la, si pagat no l'avia, e autrejar no vol la venda o ·l pens que ·l creeires far ne volria, a requesta del creedor, lo cosselh d'Agen per son offici, a requesta del creedor, somonit lo deutor que pague, o que venda, o enpenhe, si far no o vol, deu vendre lo meiss cosselhs, o enpenhar, qual que melhs pusca, aquela causa obligada per vendre o per empenhar, aissi cum predighs es; e deu ne pagar lo creedor. E si pagar no l'en pot, lo deutres es tenguts pagar lo remanent tota hora entro que pagat l'aia, e pot s'en clamar al senhor lo creeires senes enquesta. E aquela venda o aquel penhs que ·l cosselhs faria, aissi cum sobre dighs es, d'aquela causa per neceira del deutor, auria tant bona fermetat cum si lo deutres o vendia e (sic, for o?) o enpen- [f. 49r] -hava pero si lo creeires per lo poder que ·l deutres l'en auria dat o volia vendre o enpenhar per falha del deutor, del terme establit entre lui e ·l deutor en la pot o far, e auria tant bona fermetat cum si lo deutres o ·l cosselhs o vendia o o enpenhava, lo deutor equeregut, e facha la dicha crida. E ·l cosseilhs deu i dar sa auctoritat, e o deu cofermar ab carta publica e ab lo sagel comunal d'Agen pendent en aquela carta.

[CHAPTER XXV]

Negus hom d'Agen no deu ni es tenguts autrejar maio, ni terra, ni vinha, ni neguna possessio, ni heretat que hom tenga de lui a feus, a gleia, ni a maio d'orde, ni de religio, ni a clerc, ni a cavoer, ni a Jueu. E si o fazia, o en qualque manera alcuna possessios o heretats que fos de la costuma d'Agen avengues a gleia, o a maio d'orde, o de religio, o a cavoer, o a clerc, o a Jueu, o per compra, o per conquesta, [f.49v] o per sucessio, o per heretatge, o per als, si dints un an e un mes no avia venduda aquela honor, lo senher del feus, de l'an e ·l mes en la, pot prendre son feus, e pot lo tener, e uzar, e espleitar tant longament entro aquela honors sia venduda a feuzater laic.

[CHAPTER XXVI]

Aci parla de prescriptio per longa tenezo de temps.

Negus hom ni neguna femna no pot demandar per negu dreghs, ni per neguna razo, ni en neguna manera, de .xxx. ans en la, maio, ni terra, ni vinha, ni cazal, ni

Since many men owe debts, as security for which they place houses or land or some other real property [*honor*] in the jurisdiction of the lord, it has long [f. 48v] been the ancient practice [*uzage*] in Agen, that if someone owes a debt to another per- son, for which he has given a house, or land, or some other real property [*honor*] as security under the jurisdiction of the lord of that fief, and has given him, if he has not paid, the power to sell it or use it as security from the due date of payment of the debt forward, and will not authorize the sale or the use as security [*pens*] that the creditor wanted to proceed with, {then} at the request of the creditor the council of Agen, in its official capacity [*de son offici*], at the request of the creditor, when the debtor has been summoned to pay or sell or give {the property} as security [*empenha*], {and} if he will not, the said council should sell or mortgage [*empenhar*] (whichever it can more easily do) the property that is pledged to be sold or mortgaged [*empenhar*], as is said above. And {the council} should pay the creditor out of it. And if it cannot pay him out of the proceeds, the debtor is obligated for ever to pay the remainder, until he has paid it, and the creditor can lodge a complaint with the lord without having to make an attempt at settlement [*senes enquesta*]. And the sale or mortgage [*penhs*] that the council made as said above of that property because of the need of the debtor would be as firm as if the debtor {himself} sold the property or mortgaged it [f. 49r] (but if the creditor, by the power that the debtor had given him, wanted to sell or mortgage it because of the default of the debtor on and beyond the due date established between him and the debtor, he can do so, and it would have the same firmness as if the debtor or the council had sold it or mortgaged it), once the debtor had been offered a settlement [*enqueregut*] and the said announcements made. And the council should give its authority, and confirm {the creditor's action} with a public instrument [*carta publica*], and with the seal of the commune of Agen appended to the instru– ment.

[CHAPTER XXV]

No man of Agen should or must hand over a house or land nor a vineyard nor any property, nor land {any of which is} held from him as a fief, to a monastery or a house belonging to an order, nor to a religious house, nor to a clerk, a knight or a Jew. And if he did, or in whatever {other} manner some property or land [*heretats*] under the custom of Agen has come into the possession of a monastery or a house belonging to an order, or a religious house, or a knight or a clerk or a Jew, whether by purchase or other acquisition [*conquesta*], [f. 49v] or by succession or inheritance, or some other way, {and} if within a year and a month {the new possessor} has not sold that real property [*honor*], {then} after a year and a month or more the lord of the fief can take his fief, and can hold it and use it [*uzar*] and exploit it for as long as that property [*honors*] is not sold to a secular fiefholder.

[CHAPTER XXVI]

Here it tells of prescription[31] by holding over a long period.

No man or woman can sue for [*demandar*] under any law or for any reason in any way from 30 years forward a house or land or a vineyard or a building plot [*cazal*] or

oblias, ni autra heretat o possessio, qualsque sia, que hom o femna d'Agen aia, [f. 50r] ni tenga, ni possedisca, ni aia tengut, ni agut, ni possedit en bona possessio, cum la sua causa, .xxx. ans o plus senes fadiament de dreghs. Salb que penhs pot hom tot dia demandar, que possessios ni tenezos de .xxx. ans, ni de mais ni de menhs, nozer ni prejudicar no li pot. Quar penhs tener no es vertadeirament possedir; e salb que possessios no pot nozer de fraire contra fraire, quant que tenga l'us o l'autre las heretats e causas comunals entre fraires, entro que aio partit lors heretats e lors bes, aissi que cadaus sapja sa part.

[CHAPTER XXVII]

Enapres digam de causas dadas en dot, o per razo de dot, cals costuma n'es. [f. 50v]

De causas dadas en dot deu estre defenit segont los covents que seran enpres en las espozalhas, so es en las fermalhas del matremoni, pero tota heretats e tota causa que sia dada per honor segont la costuma d'Agen en dot deu tornar a tot home o a tota femna que plus pres deura heretar en las causas de la molher, si ela muria avant que sos marits senes heret que de lor matrimoni non remazes. E si ·l marits muria avant que la molher, la molher cobraria sa honor souta e [f. 51r] quita, e son aver e sas causas que auria portat a son marit, o n'agues heret o no. E si es pucela, lo marits lo deu doblar son aver moble, so es los diners o las dinaradas que aura agut per leis o de leis en dot estimadas, si la molher muria avant que ·l marits senes heret que no agues, o agut no agues, de leiss, si exceptat no es a las espozalhas; mas pero si, aissi cum predighs es, alcuna terra o causa es dada per honor ad alcu ab molher en dot, lo marits pot aver, e tener, e possedir, e uzar, e espletar aquela honor tant quant ab aquela sa molher viura essemps e apres, pero senes tot alienament ans deu tornar apres la mort del marit a la molher, si viva es, o a son heret si n'a de son matrimoni, o a tota persona que [f. 51v] els bes de leiss plus pres deura heretar, senes que longa tenezos de .xxx. ans ni de mais ni de menhs en aital cas no prescriu ni nots ni prejudica.

[CHAPTER XXVIII][32]

Lo senher no deu nulhs temps traire ostatges ni demandar de la vila d'Agen, de la ciutat, ni dels borcs, ni tort ni forsa no deu far als ciutadas ni als borzes d'Agen, ni outra lors costumas no los deu anar el ni hom per lui; ni negu home en la vila d'Agen no deu prendre, ni defora, que sia ciutadas ni borzes d'Agen, si no o fazia per jutga-

{a right to}quit-rent [*oblias*], or any other piece of real propert or possession whatever, that a man or woman of Agen has [f. 50r] or holds or possesses, and has held or had or possessed in good possession, as his {or her} own property for 30 years or more without challenge [*fadiament*] in court. Except that you can always sue on mortgaged property [*penhs*], because holding or possession of more or less than thirty years cannot prevent or prejudice you. For to hold mortgaged property is not truly to possess it. And an exception is that possession does not prevent a suit of brother against brother, however long one or the other holds real property and {other} property held in common by brothers, until they have made a partition of their inheritance and their wealth [*bes*] so that each one will know what is his share.

[CHAPTER XXVII]

Following this let us speak of what the custom is concerning things given as a dowry, or by reason of a dowry. [f. 50v]

Things given in a dowry must be dealt with [*defenit*] according to the agreement made at the espousal, that is, in the marriage contract, for all inherited property and any property given as real property [*honor*] in dowry according to the custom of Agen should go back to any man or woman who should inherit the property of the wife, as the next of kin, if she dies before her husband, without an heir remaining from their marriage. And if the husband died before the wife, the wife would get back her real property [*honor*] free and [f. 51r] clear of debt, and her wealth [*aver*] and her {tangible} personal property she brought to the marriage, whether she had an heir by him or not. And if she was a virgin, the husband should double her personal property, that is the money or value in money [*dinaradas*] he had received for her or from her as a dowry, as estimated, {and} if the wife died before the husband without an heir she had or had had by him, unless an exception is made in the marriage contract.[33] But nevertheless if as above said any land or property [*causa*] is given as dowry land [*honor*] to someone with a woman as a dowry, {then} the died before the husband without an heir she had or had had by him, unless an exception is made in the marriage contract.[34] But nevertheless if as above said any land or property [*causa*] is given as Dowry land [*honor*] to someone with a woman as a dowry, {then} the husband can have and hold and possess and use and exploit that land [*honor*] as long as he lives together with that wife, and afterwards, but without alienating it; instead it must go back after the husband's death to the wife if she is alive, or to her heir if she has one from her marriage, or to any person who [f. 51v] can inherit her property as next of kin, without the long term holding of 30 years, or more or less, preserving or harming or prejudicing {their rights} in this case.

[CHAPTER XXVIII]

The lord must never take or demand hostages from the city of Agen, from the city or the suburbs [*borcs*] and he must not do harm or use force on the citizens or bourgeois of Agen, nor may he infringe their customs, neither he nor any man for him. And he may not arrest [*prendre*] in the city of Agen, or outside, any man who is a citizen or bourgeois of Agen, unless he does so by a judgment of the council and

ment del cosselh e dels proshomes d'Agen. Ni deu far lo senher a Agen castel nul temps. E tughs li home d'Agen son e estre devo franc a Lafodz[35] ab totas lors causas, e per [f. 52r] tota la terra de la senhoria de Bouvila,[36] de tots peatges, e de totas leidas, e de totas costumas, e de totas exactios que hom i aia levat sa en reire ni i levara per enant. E totas mercadarias, sio blats, o vis, o autras causas, devo passar home d'Agen per tota la terra del senher prince vas ont que sia per lo dreghs peatge ancianament acostumat. E tots hom d'Agen deu passar a Marmanda[37] ab .iiii. diners de peatge del tonel de vi, e ab un diner de la conca de blat, d'ont que sia lo blats ni ·l vis, e tota autra mercadaria deu passar ab lo dreghs peatge ancia. E tots hom qui compre blat ni vi d'Agen deu passar a Marmanda, aissi cum sobre dighs es, ab .iiii. diners del tonel de vi, e ab un diner de la conca del blat. [f. 52v]

[CHAPTER XXIX]

Aquest capitols qui ve apres parla qual franqueza a lo cosselhs d'Agen de far establiments entre ·ls habitants del meiss loc.

Lo cosselhs d'Agen pot far ab los proshomes del meiss loc establiments a Agen, e en sos apertenements, li qual devo durar e tener tant cum al cosselh plaira, e no plus, aissi cum li cosselhs e li prohome d'Agen conoisseran que sia lo profeghs de la vila e dels habitants, sobre batezos e sobre mals dighs e sobre autras malas fachas que desobre no son expressadas, cum d'intrar en l'autrui ort, e en la autrui vinha, o metre bestiari en l'autrui prat en temps de defes, e d'au- [f. 53r] -tras causas e i pot lo cosselhs ab los proshomes d'Agen establir gatges quals se volha a son bon albire per castiament de las gents, quar pluzors vegadas pena et gatges, quant los leva d'aquels qui fan ad autrui o en la causa d'autrui aquo que no volria que hom fes a lui ni en sa causa, refreno mants homes de mal, los quals la paors de Deu de mal far no revoca, e d'aquels gatges pot dar lo cosselhs tant quant se volra al senhor, per que ·l senher sia ajudaires al cosselh a mantener e a defendre lors establiments.

[CHAPTER XXX]

En aquest capitol conseguents parla en qual manera hom pot logar maio a Agen e quals es la costuma del loguer. [f. 53v]

Tots hom pot logar sa maio a Agen a cui se volra per sa meissa auctoritat, a terme saubut, e l'estatgers deu tener aquela maio per tot lo terme que logada l'aura, senes que ·l senher de la maio tolre no la i pot per autrui, tant quant l'en pagara so loguer aissi cum entre lor sera enpres, si no o fazia per la propria estatja, o per tener sas causas proprias, e d'aquo pot aver l'estatgers sagrament del senhor de la maio que propriament per sa estatja o per sas proprias causas la vol e l'a ops, e que tot aquel terme que l'aura logada ad aquel estatger la tenra a sos ops senes que no i metra autre estatger tot [f. 54r] aquel terme que l'aura logada. E si l'estatgers no paga al senhor de

goodmen of Agen. Nor may the lord construct a castle at any time in Agen. And all the men of Agen, throughout the lands of the lordship of Beauville, are and must be free at Lafox with all their property [f. 52r] of all tolls and payments [*leidas*] and of all customary dues and all exactions that have been levied in the past, or will be levied in the future. And a man of Agen must pass all {his} merchandise, whether it be wheat or wine or other things, throughout all the lands of the principal lord [*senher prince*] in any direction, according to the lawful toll that {has been} customary {since} of old. And any man from Agen must pass through Marmande {by paying} a toll of 4 den–iers per barrel of wine and one denier per *conca* of wheat, wherever the wheat or the wine came from, and all other merchandise must pay the lawful ancient toll. And any man that buys wheat or wine in Agen should pass through Marmande {by pay–ing}as said above 4 deniers per barrel of wine and one denier per *conca* of wheat. [f. 52v]

CHAPTER XXIX]

This chapter which comes below tells of what power [*franqueza*] the council of Agen has to make statutes [*establiments*] among the residents of the said place.

The council of Agen, with the goodmen of the said place and its outlying lands [*apertenements*] can make statutes in Agen. They must remain in force [*durar*] as long as the council wishes, and no longer, as the council and the goodmen of Agen decide [*conoisseran*] will be for the good of the town, and the residents, concerning batteries [*batezos*] and defamation, and other offenses that are not expressed above, such as entering another person's garden, or vineyard, or putting cattle into someone else's meadow at times when it is not permitted, and other [f. 53r] things. And the coun- cil, with the goodmen of Agen, can establish any fines [*gatges*] it wants in its good [*albire*], judgment for the deterrence of people. For many times, punishment and fines, when they are extracted from those who do to others or to other's property what they would not want to be done to themselves or to their property, deter from evil many men who are not held back from evil by the fear of God. And from these fines the council can give as much as it wishes to the lord, so that the lord will be of help to the council in maintaining and defending their statutes.

[CHAPTER XXX]

This following chapter tells how a person can rent his house in Agen, and what the customs of rental are. [f. 53v]

Any man can, on his own authority, rent out his house in Agen to anyone he wants for a known term. And the occupant [*estatgers*][38] must keep the house for the whole term he rented it for, without the owner [*senher*] of the house being able to take it away from him for another person as long as he pays the rent as agreed between them, unless {the landlord} did so {took it away} for his own occupancy or to store his own things, and for this the renter can require an oath from the landlord that he wants and needs it for his own personal occupation or for his own things and that, for the whole term for which he had rented it to that occupant, he will reserve it for his use, without putting in another occupant for the whole [f. 54r] period that he had

la maio son loguer a terme o a termes establits, lo senher de la maio ne pot gitar aquel estatger e sarrar la maio ab totas las causas que l'estatgers aura en la maio, que devo estre en la sazina del meiss senhor tant entro que l'estatgers l'aia pagat son loguer e pot s'en pagar per sa propria auctoritat de las meissas causas si l'estatgers en autra manera pagar no ·l pot son loguer. E quant venra a la fi del terme, l'estatgers deu venir al senhor de la maio per .viii. dias avant, e deu lo dire que queira autre estatger en la maio, o ·n fassa sa voluntat; e dints los meiss .viii. dias deu l'estatgers dezenbargar la maio de sas cauzas de [f. 54v] manera que al dia establit la aia dezenbargada, e que al meiss dia lo reda o l'aia reduda la clau de la maio. E si no o fazia, aquela maios es logada ad aquel estatger un autre an continuable, per meiss for e per meiss loguer, on pagara l'estatgers al senhor de la maio son loguer per los covents de l'autre an passat, si estar i vol o no vol, e aquo es en la volontat del senhor de la maio, si vol que aquel estatgers la retenga o no; pero si ·l senher de la maio per sa propria estatja, o per sas cauzas tener, la dicha maio, aissi cum predighs es, dints lo terme retenia, deu o far a ssaber a l'estatger per .viii. dias avant que l'en gite, per ostar sas cauzas, e per sercar autra maio, e si l'estatgers l'en deu re del loguer, no [f. 55r] li es tenguts pagar, ni ·l senher de la maio ni autre destrenher no l'en pot. E si l'estatgers fazia ab volontat del senhor de la maio obra nesessaria en la maio, devo caher las despessas que i faria del loguer, e ·l senher de la maio es lo tenguts redre lo menhs falhent, si aquo que l'estatgers lo deuria del loguer no i abastava. E si re en la maio l'estatgers afolava, deu o esmendar al senhor de la maio a esgart del cosselh. ¶ Negus hom qui aia logada maio d'autrui a Agen no la pot logar ad autrui per que aquel estatger balhe al senhor de la maio per son estatger, senes volontat del meiss senhor; pero lo senher de la maio a aquel estatger que l'autre lo balhara, si ·l recep, re no pusca de- [f. 55v] -mandar mas tant quant lo primers l'en deura de loguer. Mas si ·l primers estatgers i metia autre estatger senes que al senhor de la maio no ·l presentes per estatger, lo primers estatgers es tenguts pagar ad aquel senhor tot lo loguer entegrament, senes tot plaghs, e senes tota exceptio, si l'autre s'en fugia, o pagar no ·l podia.

[CHAPTER XXXI]

Conseguentre cove que digam cum lo cosselhs d'Agen a poder de destrenher tot ciutada o borzes d'Agen de pagar a son sirvent o a sa sirventa son loguer o sa soldada que covent l'aura, si n'a rancurant.

S'alcus hom o alcuna femna ve rancurants o rancuranta al cosselh d'alcu ciutada [f. 56r] o borzes d'Agen, que per son loguer o per sa soldada re lo deia e pagar no lo vol, lo cosselhs deu destrenher aquel ciutada o borzes de pagar, senes que ·l senher no i a gatge, si clamant agut no n'avia.

rented it for. And if the renter does not pay his rent to the owner of the house at the appointed time or times, the owner can evict the renter and lock the house with all the renter's property in the house, which must remain in the possession [*sazina*] of the said owner until the renter has paid him his rent. And he can pay himself on his own authority from the said property if the renter cannot pay him his rent in any other way. And when the end of the rental period comes, the renter must come to the owner of the house 8 days before and should say to him that he should seek another renter for the house, or do whatever he wants, and within the said 8 days the renter must empty the house of his property so that [f. 54v] he has emptied it on the established day, and that on the said day he returns or has returned the key of the house. And if he did not do so, that house is rented to that renter for another year on the same terms [*for*] and for the same rent, so that the renter will pay the owner of the house his rent according to the agreement for the previous year, whether he wants to live there or not. And it is at the will of the owner whether that renter keeps the house or not. But if as before said the owner of the house reserved the said house for his own occupancy or to store his property within the rental period, he must inform the renter 8 days before he evicts him, so that he can remove his property and look for another house. And if the renter owed him any of the rent, he is not [f. 55r] obliged to pay him, and neither the owner of the house nor anyone else can make him do so. And if the renter, with the agreement of the owner, did any necessary work on the house, the expenses he incurred must be deducted from the rent; and the owner of the house is required to reimburse him the difference if what the renter owed on the rent was not enough. And if the renter damaged anything in the house, he must make it up to the owner at the estimation of the council. ¶ No man who has rented someone else's house in Agen can rent it to someone else so that he gives the owner of the house that person as his renter, without the permission of the said owner; but the owner cannot ask [f. 55v] anything of that {new} renter whom the previous renter gave him, if he accepts him, except what the other renter owed him as rent. But if the first renter put in another occupant without presenting him as a renter to the owner of the house, the first renter is required to pay the owner the entire rent, without any lawsuit, and without any defense, if the other renter runs away or cannot pay him.

[CHAPTER XXXI]

Following this it is right that we tell how the council of Agen has the power to oblige any citizen or bourgeois of Agen to pay to his man or woman servant the wages or salary he has agreed to, if there is a complaint.

If some man or woman brings a complaint before the council of Agen concerning some citizen [f. 56r] or bourgeois of Agen, {saying} that he owes them something on their wages or salary, and will not pay, the council should force the citizen or bourgeois to pay it, without the lord getting a fine if he had not received a complaint [*si clamant agut no n'avia*].

[CHAPTER XXXII]

Aquest capitols parla cum li ciutada e li borzes d'Agen podo far bastidas en lors proprietats.

Tots ciutadas e tots borzes d'Agen pot far bastida en sa proprietat, e i pot metre costumas e establiments, salvas las senhorias e las drechuras del senhor principal de la terra. So es a ssaber que ·l senher d'aquela bastida deu far ost al prince totas vets que la ciutats d'Agen [f. 56v] e l'autra terra lo fara ost, la qual ost lo deu far per si e per los homes d'aquela bastida, e li home d'aquel loc son quiti de la ost del prince per la ost del senhor d'aquela bastida.

[CHAPTER XXXIII]

E en aquest capitol parla dels avenediss, so es a ssaber dels homes defora qui veno estar a Agen, quals costuma n'es.

Quant hom deforas ve a Agen per estre ciutadas o borzes del meiss loc, deu primerament forsjurar, toquats los sants evangelis, hyretges, e sabatats, e tota manera e tota error de hyretgia. E apres aqui meiss [f. 57r] deu jurar al senhor e al cosselh, aissi cum dighs es desobre al comensament que home d'Agen devo jurar al senhor e al cosselh, e deu metre el sagrament que estara a dreghs a esgart del senhor e del cosselh a tots sos rancurants, e que dints un an e un mes comprara a Agen maio, o terra, o vinha, o autra heretat segont son poder, a esgart del cosselh. E deu estre quitis e francs aquel an e aquel mes d'ost, e de gacha, e de tota messio de vila quant, aissi cum predighs es, aura jurat. E quant tals avenediss sera venguts a Agen, cum que toque a la.i. dels portals del meiss loc, lo senher del loc dont aquel avenediss sera venguts ni autre no ·l deu prendre, ni mal far a lui ni a sas causas, e si o fazia, lo senher, [f. 57v] e ·l cosselhs, e la universitat d'Agen devo enparar, e demandar, e defendre lui e sas causas cum lor ciutada o lor borzes. ¶Item si aitals avenediss te feus a oblias e acaptes, o ad autres servicis, que non sia hom per feus d'omenatge, aquel avenediss deu tener e possedir aquel feus paziblament senes tot contrast que no li deu metre aquel senher ni autre, e usar e esplechar estant a Agen, ab qu'en fassa al senhor d'aquel feus sos devers que primerament per lo meiss feus lo fazia, e ·l pot dar, o vendre, o alienar a tota persona que aquel feus servisca ad aquel senhor, ab los devers que aquel far l'en devia ni l'en fazia, e ·n pot portar totas sas causas moblas a Agen, senes tota forssa e senes tot contrast [f. 58r] que aquel senher ni autre no li deu far despois que (a) Agen, aissi cum predighs es, sera venguts. E si aquel senher o autre sobre aisso molestava lui ni sas causas, lo senher, e ·l cosselhs, e la universitats d'Agen devo lui e sas causas demandar, e enparar, e defendre cum lor ciutada o lor borzes. Mas si te feus en homenatge del senhor del loc dont sera venguts e partits, o d'autrui, e ·l senher d'a-

CHAPTER XXXII]

This chapter tells of how the citizens and bourgeois of Agen can create bastides [*bastidas*] on their property.

Any citizen and any bourgeois of Agen can create a bastide on his property, and establish customs and issue regulations [*establiments*], preserving the lordship and rights of the sovereign lord of the land. That is to say that the lord of that bastide must provide military aid [*far ost*] to the sovereign every time that the city of Agen [f. 56v] and the other land provide military aid {to the sovereign}, and {the lord of the bastide} must provide this aid for himself and for the men of that bastide. And the men of that place are exempt from the prince's army because of the service of the lord of that bastide.

[CHAPTER XXXIII]

In this chapter it speaks of newcomers. That is to say, what the custom is concerning men from outside who come to settle in Agen.

When a man from outside comes to Agen to become a citizen or bourgeois of the said place, he must first, with his hand on the Holy Gospels, forswear heretics and vaudois and all manner and all errors of heresy. And afterwards, in the same place, [f. 57r] he must swear to the lord and the council, as it was said above at the beginning that men of Agen must swear to the lord and to the council, and he must include in the oath that he will appear [*estara a dreghs*] before the lord and his council at their judgment to answer all complaints against him; and that within a year and a month he will buy in Agen a house or land or a vineyard, or some other property according to his ability, at the order of the council; and for that year and a month he must be excused from military service and the watch and any city duties, when he has sworn as said above. And when such an outsider comes to Agen, such as when he knocks at one of the gates of the said place, neither the lord of the place from which the newcomer came, nor any other man, should arrest him nor do him harm personally or to his property. And if anyone did so, the lord [f. 57v] and the council and the whole community of Agen must protect and claim and defend him and his property as their citizen or their bourgeois. ¶ If such a newcomer holds a fief for quit-rent and relief, or for some other service, and he is not a man who has sworn homage [*per feus d'omenatge*] this newcomer must hold and possess the fief peacefully without any challenge from that lord or other person, and have use of it and exploit it, while a resident of Agen, provided he does to the lord of that fief the duty he had formerly been used to doing for the said fief. And he can give it as a gift or sell it or alienate it to any person who can give service for the fief to that lord, by performing the duties that he should perform or had been performing. And he can transport all his personal property to Agen, free from all force, and all challenge [f. 58r] that that lord or any other person might offer him, once he has arrived in Agen as was said before. And if that lord or any other molested him or his property concerning this, then the lord and the council and the community of Agen should claim and protect and defend him as their citizen or their bourgeois. But if he holds a fief in homage from the lord of the

quel feus d'omenatge, o hom per lui, lo trobava en aquel feus estant, so es a ssaber que i fes rezidentia, o prendent, o portant, o raubant de las causas d'aquel feus d'omenatge, e l'i pren, non es tenguts al senhor, ni al cosselh, ni als habitants d'Agen, ni ad autrui; ni ·l senher, ni ·l cosselhs ni la uni- [f. 58v] -versitats d'Agen no ·l devo enparar ni demandar, la cauza proada abondozament. Mas si passant per aquel feus, cum autre per sa cocha, senes que el meiss feus no estes, so es que no i fes rezidentia, ni no ·n prezes, ni no ·n portes de las causas del meiss feus, lo senher d'a- quel feus ni autre no ·l deu restar, ni prendre, ni ·l deu far mal. E si o fazia, lo senher, e ·l cosselhs, e la universitats d'Agen lo devo demandar e enparar cum lor ciutada o lor borzes.

[CHAPTER XXXIV]

Enapres cove que digam de testaments e dels heretatges dels efants.

Tots hom d'Agen pot far orde e testament dels bes e de las causas que aura, [f. 59r] salb que terra ni heretat de linhatge negus hom no pot dar ni laissar a negu home, ni a neguna femna, salb ad aquel o ad aquels que plus propri torner ne seran del linhatge per lo qual aquela heretats sera venguda; mas diners i pot dar o laissar desobre, ab que la causa valha mais lo quart, pero be pot hom dar e laissar en son testament per amor Deu e de sa arma en tot e en partida a sa volontat sas causas moblas e no-moblas, en qualque manera las possedisca cum suas, si heret no a de son matrimoni. Mas negus hom d'Agen no deu ni pot dezeretar sos enfants dels bes que aia per son linhatge, o per proprietat, o per conquesta de si meiss, per que sos enfants no laisse hereters els meiss bes, [f. 59v] son orde e sos deutes pagats, si cas d'aquels dels quals dreghs parla per los quals paire pot dezeretar son fil no i avenia. Mas be ne pot far avantatge a l'au de sos efants plus que a l'autre, pero si a filha o filhas, pot los laissar o dar maridatge a sa volontat, e d'aquo devo estre las filhas a las quals lo paire aura dat o laissat o assignat segont sa volontat de sos bes o sobre sos bes, o las quals aura maridadas en sa vita, d'aquo que dat o promes los aura en maridatge aondozas, que els autres bes del paire re demandar no podo, ni plus aver non devo per torn, ni per successio, ni per deflaghs {*sic*}, ni per negu dreghs, ni per neguna razo, ni en neguna manera tant quant i aia autres filhs o [f. 60r] filhas, o filh o filha, del matrimoni d'aquel paire, o heret del matrimoni d'aquels, si ·l paire no los dava del seu. E per meissa manera es dighs si ·l paire marida filha en sa vita, si a tot filhas e no filh ni filhs mascles, aquela maridada deu estre aondoza d'aquo que ·l paire l'aura dat, o promes, o assignat en maridatge, que re els autres bes del paire demandar no pot, tant quant i aia neguna de

place he left and came from, or from some other person, and the lord of that homage fief or someone on his behalf found him residing in that fief, that is to say making his home there or harvesting [*prendent*] or taking things away [*portant*] or robbing the property belonging to that fief in homage, and he {the lord of the fief} arrested him [*li pren*], then {that lord} is not obligated [*tenguts*] to the lord or to the council nor to the inhabitants of Agen or anyone else, and the lord and the council and the [f. 58v] community of Agen should not protect or claim him, once the thing has been abundantly proved. But if he is passing through the fief with someone else on his business, without being domiciled on the said fief, that is to say that he had not established his home there, and was not harvesting or taking away any of the property of the said fief, then neither the lord of that fief nor any other person should arrest him or capture him or do him harm. And if they did, the lord and the council and the community of Agen should claim and protect him as their citizen or their bourgeois.

[CHAPTER XXXIV]

And after this it is right for us to tell of wills and of the inherited property of children.

Any man of Agen can make a will [*orde*] and testament concerning the wealth and property that he may have. [f. 59r] Except that no man can give or leave land or family property to any man or woman except to the person or persons who are the closest remaindermen [*torner*] of the family from which the land came to him; but he can give or leave money in addition [*desobre*], even if the property was worth more than a quarter {of his wealth}. But a man can give and leave at will in his testament, for the love of God and for his own soul, in whole or in part, his personal property, and real property, in whatever manner he possesses them as his own, if he has no heir from his marriage. But no man of Agen can or should disinherit his children of the things he has through his family, either from inherited ownership [*proprietat*] or that he has himself acquired, in such a way that his children do not inherit the said wealth, [f. 59v] once his will has been executed and his debts paid, unless there arose one of the cases spoken of by law, through which a father can disinherit his son. But he can give more of his wealth to one of his children than to another. But if he has a daughter or daughters, he can leave or give a dowry as he pleases, and the daughters to whom the father has given or left or assigned some of his property in his will, or in addition to the property with which he married them in his lifetime, should be satisfied [*aondozas*] with what he gave them or promised them as a dowry, for they cannot ask for any of the rest of their father's property, and they should not get more as a remainder or by succession or by undoing [*def(l)aghs*] {of the will}[39] nor through any other law or reason, nor in any manner, as long as there are other sons or [f. 60r] daughters, or one son or one daughter, from the marriage of that father, or an heir of the marriage of one of them, unless the father gave them some of his own property [*del seu*]. And the same thing is said if the father marries off a daughter in his lifetime: if he has all daughters and no male son or sons, that married daughter should be satisfied with what the father gave or promised her or assigned her as a dowry, so that she cannot ask for any of her father's other property as long as there are any of the

las autras filhas o heret de lor matrimoni, si ·l paire no lo dava. Empero si ·l paire moria senes testament, o senes orde, sas filhas si n'avia heretario els bes del paire per egals partidas ab lors fraires que aurio per lo paire, esters aquela que ·l paire auria maridada, pero els bes de la maire devo [f. 60v] las filhas heretar per engals partidas ab los fraires, salb d'aquela que seria maridada durant lo matrimoni entre ·l paire e la maire, si de las causas de la maire re agut avia que la maire l'agues dat o assignat en dot, vivents lo paire e la maire. E maire no pot dezeretar sos efants que no remango hereter en sos bes, pagat son orde e sos deutes, mas be ne pot far avantatge a la u[40] plus que a l'autre. ¶Item: si heretats es dada a Agen en maridatge, e la femna ab la qual la heretats es dada a heret d'aquel marit, e ·l marits mor avant que ela, e pren autre marit del qual aia heret, aquela heretats es del heret del derrer marit apres la mort de leiss, soutament senes que ·l heret del primer marit here- [f. 61r] -tar no i pot, si la maire aquela heretat a dada al derrer marit en dot estimada per prets d'aver per far sas volontats. Mas si la i a dada per honor segont la costuma d'Agen, tughs li heret del primer marit e del derrer i devo heretar per engals partidas, salb que a sa fi ne pot la maire far avantatge a l'au plus que a l'autre. Ni neguna femna que paires a ja maridada, ab la qual lo paire aia dada heretat o causa per honor segont la costuma d'Agen, no deu ni pot dar ni laissar de la meissa causa, ni aver desobre, a marit, ni a home, ni a femna, ni a negu loc, ni ·n pot far neguna causa per que als plus propis herets de leiss no torne soutament apres sa mort. Mas tota femna que remanga apres la mort de [f. 61v] son paire que no sia estada maridada pot far donatio e laissa sobre las causas en las quals remanria hereteira per son paire, o que ·l seran avengudas per successio, en la forma e en la manera que es dighs desobre el comensament d'aquest capitol, cum hom pot far do o laissa sobre terra de linhatge. E si alcus que aia alcunas heretats, o possessios, o autras causas conquestas que no fosso de son linhatge, mor senes heret de son matrimoni, pot ne far sa volontat senes torn que hom ni femna no i a per succession de lui, si no mor intestatus, quar aissi i auria lo linhatges de lui son torn. E es a ssaber que hom pot far testament e orde quant aia .xiiii. ans d'etat, e no d'aqui en aval e femna a .xii. ans e no d'aqui en jos. [f. 62r]

[CHAPTER XXXV]

Aquest capitols parla de veuzas, e d'orfanhols, e de menors d'etat, qual razo an a demandar lor dreghs per la costuma d'Agen.

Veuzas e orfanhols e menors de .xxv. ans podo demandar lor razo segont que dreghs vol, pero si alcuna heretats o possessios que fos d'alcuna molher era venduda estant ab lo marit que auria, e aquel marit mort, si la molher lo sobrevivia, aquela molher aquela causa no demandava o no calonjava dints .xxx. ans dels meiss .xxx. ans a en la es prescriut contra leiss, que d'aqui en la redemandar no i pot, ni si ela la sua

other daughters, or heirs from their marriage, if their father left her nothing. How–ever, if the father died without a will or testament, his daughters if he had any would inherit their father's property in equal shares with their brothers of the same father, except the daughter that the father had married off. But the daughters [f. 60v] must inherit property coming from their mother in equal shares with their brothers, except a sister who had been married off during the marriage of her father and mother, if she had received any of her mother's property, which her mother had given her or assigned her as a dowry when her father and mother were both alive. And a mother may not disinherit her children so that they are not the inheritors of her property, once her will has been executed and her debts paid, but she can give more to one than to ano-ther. ¶Item, if a piece of land is given in Agen as a dowry, and the woman with whom the land is given has an heir by that husband, and the husband dies before her, and she takes another husband by whom she has an heir, that land belongs freely to the heir of the later husband after her death, so that the heir of the first husband cannot [f. 61r] inherit it, if the mother has given that land to the second husband in dowry, estimated as to its worth in money to do with as he wishes [*estimada per prets d'aver per far sa voluntat*]. But if she gave it as an a piece of dowry real property [*per honor*] according to the custom of Agen, all the heirs of the first husband and the second should inherit in equal shares. Except that on her death [*a sa fi*] the mother can give more to one than to another. And a woman whom her father had already married off, with whom the father gave land or other property as dowry real property [*per honor*] according to the custom of Agen cannot and must not give away or leave that property, or any money in addition, to her husband, nor to any man or woman or place [*loc*], nor do anything with it by which it does not come as a remainder to her closest kin immediately after her death. But any woman who, after the death of [f.61v] her father, had not been married off can make a gift or bequest from the property of which she was her father's heir, or which came to her by succession, in the form and manner described above at the beginning of this chapter about how a person can make a gift or bequest of the land belonging to his family [*linhatge*]. And if someone who had some land or possessions or other acquired property that had not come from his family died without an heir from his marriage he can do what he wants with it, with no remainder to any man or woman by succession from him, unless he dies *intestatus*; for in that case the family would get a remainder. And it should be known that a man can make a will and testament when he is 14 years old, and no less [*en aval*],[41] and a woman at 12 years, and not under [*en jos*]. [f. 62r]

[CHAPTER XXXV]

This chapter tells of widows and orphans and minors, {and} what reason they have to sue for their rights according to the custom of Agen.

Widows and orphans and those under 25 years of age can sue according to law, but if some land or possession belonging to a woman was sold when she was with her hus–band, and once that husband died, that woman (if she outlived him) did not sue to get that property or challenge ownership within 30 years or less, it is protected from her, so that she cannot sue for it from then on. But if she and her husband

causa vent ab son marit [f. 62v] e jura que no venga encontra, re demandar no i pot, per que lo sagrament aia faghs de son grat senes tota forssa.

[CHAPTER XXXVI]

De causa jutgada per lo cosseilh d'Agen, si hom venia encontra parla aquest capitols.

Si neguna de las partidas anava contra ·l jutgament del cosselh de cauza jutgada per lo meiss cosselh ab dels[42] proshomes d'Agen entre alcunas partidas, lo balles deu al somoniment del cosselh penhorar aquela partida rebella, e la deu destrenher de tener e complir lo jutgament del cosselh, e ·n deu tant be aver son gatge cum si a lui clamats s'en era. [f. 63r]

[CHAPTER XXXVII]

Poissas que d'autras mezuras es tractat desobre parla en aquest capitol de la mezura, so es a ssaber de la perja ab que hom perja terra a Agen, quals costuma n'es.

La mezura, so es la perja ab que hom perja terra, deu aver de lonc .xii. pes que monto .viii. razas comunals, o .viii. razas que monto .xii. pes comunals. E la dinarada de la terra deu aver si es en .iiii. caires .xii. perjas de cada part, o si es redonda deu aver .xlviii. perjas en redon. E deu la terra estre mezurada e perjada [f. 63v] ab proshomes d'Agen, e ·l perjaires deu jurar sobre sants evangelis que leialment perge, e que no i fassa per amic ni per enemic, ni per do, ni per promessa, ni per re mas la vertat e leialtat, tant be per l'una part cum per l'autra. E deu aver dints los dex d'Agen de la dinarada si non i a .iii. dinaradas o d'aqui en sus .iiii. diners de perjaduras de cada dinarada; e si n'i a mais de .iii. dinaradas, non deu aver mas .ii. diners de la dinarada. Mas si foras los dex lo mena hom per perjar terra o vinha, deu s'en aquel qui ·l menara acordar ab lui, e si dezacort i avia, deu ne aver a esgart del cosselh, segont que ·l locs sera lonh o pres. ¶Item: lo senher de feus deu e pot far perjar terra o vinha que hom tenga de lui a feus coras [f. 64r] que ·s volha, ab que i apele lo feuzater, e deu pagar lo perjador, e si mais i troba que autrejat no l'en aura primerament a feus, e a terra, o vinha que se tenga ab aquela, tot aquo mais que i seria es al senhor del feus, ab tot quant faghs i auria, si ·l senher laissar no lo volia; mas aquo es en volontat d'aquel senhor, si o vol retener o laissar. E si menhs i trobava, deu caer de las oblias e dels acaptes per razo que menhs i auria. Mas si lo senher del feus no i avia terra que ·s tengues ab aquela, e mais i trobava hom, aquo mais no pot lo senher retener, ans es del feuzater ab creissensa d'oblias e d'acaptes que ·l feuzaters l'en fassa per razo del plus, e que l'en pague per tant quant mais i auria, [f. 64v] per razo dels primers

sell her property [f. 62v] and she swears that she will not challenge it, she cannot sue for anything, provided that she has sworn the oath willingly without any force.

[CHAPTER XXXVI]

This chapter tells of a case decided by a judgment [*causa jutgada*] by the council of Agen, if it were challenged.

If any of the parties went against the judgment of the council in a matter judged by the said council with some of the goodmen of Agen between some parties, the *balle* should at the summons of the council seize property [*penhorar*] from the resisting [*rebella*] party, and should compel him to keep and carry out the judgment of the council, and {the *balle*} can collect his fine as if he had made a complaint to him. [f.63v]

[CHAPTER XXXVII]

Since other measuring units [*mezuras*] are dealt with above, it tells in this chapter what the custom is concerning measuring, that is concerning the perch [*peria*][43] with which land is measured in Agen.

The measuring unit, that is the perch, that is used to measure land should have a length of 12 feet equivalent to 8 common *razas*, or 8 *razas* equivalent to 12 common feet. And the denier's worth of land [*dinarada*] must measure 12 perches on each side if it has four right angles [*caires*] and if it is round it should be 48 perches around. And the land must be measured with the perch [f. 63v] by goodmen of Agen, and the perch-man [*periaires*] must swear on the Holy Gospels that he will measure honestly, and that he will not do it {differently} for friend or for foe, nor for a gift or a promise, nor for anything except the truth and fairness [*lialtat*], as much for one as for the other party. And within the bounds of Agen he must get {be paid} 4 deniers in measuring fees [*periuradas*] per denier's worth of land if there are three denier's worth or fewer, and if there are more than three denier's worth, he should get no more than 2 deniers per denier's worth. But if he is taken outside the limits to measure land or vineyards, the person who takes him must make an agreement with him; and if they were in disagreement, he would be paid at the estimate of the council, according to whether the place is close by or far away. ¶Item, the lord of a fief can and should measure his land or vineyards held from him as a fief whenever [f. 64r] he likes, provided he calls in the fiefholder, and he must pay the perch-man. And if he finds more than he originally gave him as a fief, and as land or vineyards that go with it, all the extra that was there would go {back} to the lord, along with anything he had done there, unless the lord wanted to leave it with him, but that is at the will of that lord, whether he wants to take it or leave it. And if he found less {land}, he should reduce the quit-rent and the relief in proportion to how much less there was. But if the lord of the fief did not have any adjoining land, and found some extra, the lord cannot keep the extra, but the fiefholder gets it with an increase of the quit-rent and of the relief the fiefholder owed because of the extra, and he should pay it according to how much extra there was [f. 64v] in proportion to the first entry fees [*intratges*] he

intratges que dat l'en auria, si intratges i avia quant fo afeuzat. E per meissa manera cum sobre dighs es, si ·l feuzaters vol reconoisser vinha o terra que tenga a feus d'autrui, pot la far perjar, lo senhor del feus semonit, e ·l feuzaters deu pagar lo perjador, e ·l senher deu i estre, o hom per lui, pero si .xxx. ans passavo, que ·l feuzaters aquo que mais i seria trobat agues tengut e possedit .xxx. ans o plus, d'aqui en la es prescriut contra aquel senhor, que re el ni autre no ·i pot de–mandar mas creissensa d'oblias e d'acaptes per razo que plus i auria que lu ·n fara lo feuzaters, ni ·l senher non es tenguts al feuzater del menhs si menhs i a. E si ·l feuzaters qui primerament [f. 65r] la cauza aura receubuda a feus o a vendut ad autrui, o alienat en alcuna manera, e menhs i avia que al primer feuzater no aura autrejat a feus, aquo menhs no es tenguts lo senher del feus perfar, ni no es tenguts portar garentia de proprietat, ni de part[44] senhoria ad aquel que del primer feuzater agut o aura, salb que al primer feuzater n'es tenguts tant solament e no ad autrui.

[CHAPTER XXXVIII]

Tot enaissi cum de las drechuras del senhor principal es tractat desobre, es ops que hom sapja quals dreghs an en lors feus ni per lors feus aquil dels quals hom te terras e autras possessios feuzalment a Agen e en sos apertenements, sio clerc [f. 65v] the o laic, e quals son las costumas dels feus; de las quals costumas, quar son diversas, son faghs divers capitol conseguentre l'u apres l'autre, dels quals lo primers capitols parla aissi.

Si lo feuzaters no paga al senhor del feus sas oblias que lo deura al dia establit, lo senher del feus a .v. sols d'arnaldencs de gatge sobre aquel feuzater, pero si lo senher del feus no volia prendre las oblias si ·l feuzaters las i presenta, o las i fa presentar, al dia, no i a gatge negu, ab que lo feuzaters auze jurar sobre sants evangelis que l'aia presentadas, e fachas presentar, las oblias al dia, e si ·l senher del feus dizia causa per que no li [f. 66r] devia prendre sas oblias, deu las prendre si ·l feuzaters las i presenta, ab que lo feuzaters lo done fermansa d'estar sobre aquo a l'esgart de sa cort, e sa corts deu estre de proshomes d'Agen, e dints la vila d'Agen; e si ab fermansa prendre no vol las oblias, no i a gatge, e deu lo fermar lo feuzaters per fermansa parlant si pot, e si no pot, deu lo fermar per sa ma e sobre ·l feus que te de lui, e si aissi no lo fermava lo feuzaters, lo senher del feus a .v. sols de gatge sobre lui. E ·l senher deu aver sos acaptes deguts de son feus a senhor mudant, mas en acaptes no a gatges, mas penhorar ne pot lo senher en son feus si hom no ·ls i paga a mudament de senhor. E si lo senher del feus penho- [f. 66v] -rava o metia son ban en son feus, e ·l feuzaters lo vedava penhora o n'ostava son ban, lo senher del feus a sobre lui .v. sols de gatge, si per n o fazia ab fermansa presentant de estar a dreghs a esgart de sa cort. E per

paid, if there were any when he was first enfoeoffed. And in the same manner as was said above, if the fiefholder wants to avow a vineyard or a piece of land he holds from someone else as a fief, he can have it measured, once the lord of the fief has been summoned, and the fiefholder must pay the measurer, and the lord must be present, or someone on his behalf. But if 30 years passed so that the fiefholder had for 30 years or more held and possessed the piece found to be extra, from then on he is protected from that lord, for neither {the lord] nor any one else can sue him for anything except an increase in quit-rent and relief, in proportion to how much extra there was, and which the fiefholder must pay; but the lord is not obliged to the fief–holder for the shortfall, if there was one. And if the fiefholder who first received place as a fief [f. 65r] has either sold or otherwise alienated {it} in some way and there was less than was given to the first fiefholder as a fief, the lord of the fief is not ob–liged to make it up, nor is he obliged to be a warrantor of ownership [*proprietat*] to, nor does he share lordship [*depart senhoria*] with, the person who had it from the first fiefholder, except that he is obligated to the first fiefholder and not to anyone else.

[CHAPTER XXXVIII]

Just as the rights of the sovereign lord are dealt with above, it is necessary for men to know what rights are possessed by those from whom lands and other possessions are held feudally in Agen and its outlands [*apertenements*], both on their fiefs and because of them, whether they are ecclesiastics or [f. 65v] lay persons, and what the customs are concerning fiefs. Concerning which customs, because they are various, there have been written various chapters following one after the other, the first chapter of which says this:

If the fiefholder does not pay the lord his quit-rent he owes him on the es–tablished day, the lord of the fief gets 5 arnaldenc sous as a fine from that fiefholder. But if the lord of the fief did not want to take the quit-rent if the fiefholder offered it to him, or had it offered to him, on the due date, there is no fine, provided that the fiefholder dares to swear {an oath} on the Holy Gospels that he offered the quit-rent to him, or had it offered, on the due date. And if the lord of the fief said a reason why he should not have [f. 66r] accepted his quit-rent, he should accept it if the fiefholder offers it to him there, provided the fiefholder gives him security to submit to the verdict of the court on this matter. And the court should be {com–posed} of good–men of Agen, and in the city of Agen. And if he will not accept the quit-rent with a security, there is no fine. And the fiefholder should provide a surety [*fermansa parlant*] if he can, and if he cannot, he should give security by {raising his} hand {in an oath} and upon {the security} of the land he holds from him. And if the fiefholder did not give this security, the lord of the fief gets a 5 sou fine from him. And the lord must receive the relief owed for his fief each time the lord changes, but in relief there is no fine, but the lord of the fief can make a seizure [*penhorar*] on his fief if he is not paid {his relief} at the time of a change of lord. And if the lord of the fief made a [f. 66v] seizure [*penhoraua*] or placed a ban on his fief, and the fiefholder resisted the seizure, or took off his ban, then the lord of the fief gets 5 sous as a fine, provided however he had done so without giving security to follow the verdict of the court. And the same is said if the fiefholder redeemed his property that the lord of the fief had

meissa manera es dighs si ·l feuzaters tornava penhora el feus que ·l senher del feus n'agues preza, senes licentia del senhor del feus, si no o fazia presentant fermansa d'estar a dreghs a esgart de sa cort. E tots feus qui sera venduts deu estre venduts en ma del senhor del feus, e deu ne aver aquel senhor sos capsols, so es a ssaber .i. diner covent al vendedor; pero si i avia torner qui se traiches avant que o volges per sos ops, aquel torners o deu aver denant lo senhor, o denant autrui, per tant quant autre i daria, o dat i auria; pero si lo senher lo vol retener aissi cum predighs es, deu jurar sobre ·ls [f. 67v] sants evangelis, si ·l compraires o ·l vendeires o demanda, que per sa de cada .xii. diners, e sos acaptes, senes que ·l senher del feus no deu re demandar per lo feus autrejar salb sos capsols e sos acaptes [f. 67r] tant solament; e deu lo ades autrejar al comprador senes tot perlongament. Salb aitant que si ·l meiss senher lo vol retener, pot lo per dreghs de senhoria retener denant autrui, per tant quant autre i volra dar, e pot ne aver .viii. dias continuables de cosselh, si se vol ni o demanda, e al meiss dia deu lo retener per tant quant autre i volra dar si retener lo vol, e deu ne far aquelas pagas ades o a terme, cum lo compraires auria taula o rete propriament, senes tot autre genh, e senes tota autra cubeita, e senes covent que non aia faghs de laissar ad autrui, e que ·l tenra .i. an e .i. mes continualment a sos ops; mas si torners o rete aquel, aissi cum denant lo senhor e denant autrui o pot retener, o pot vendre quant retengut o aura, e ·n pot far sa volontat coras que se volha, ab que jure sobre ·ls sants evangelis si l'es demandat que quant lo retenc, lo compret per sos ops propriament, senes tot mal genh, e senes que per autrui no ·l retenia, e aquo senes tot mal genh que no i metia. E si a la fi dels .viii. dias sobredighs lo senher del feus retener no [f. 68r] o vol, deu o ades autrejar al comprador al meiss terme senes major alongament, ab sos acaptes, e ab sos capsols qu'en aia, aissi cum predighs es, e no plus. E si autrejar no o volia al comprador aissi cum sobredighs es, lo feuzaters, so es a ssaber lo compraires o ·l vendeires qualsque se volha, s'en deu rancurar al cosselh d'Agen, e si per lo cosselh autrejar no o vol, pot s'en clamar al senher senes tota enquesta. E si tornes, so es a ssaber hom o femna que fos del parentat dont lo feus agues estat, no se traia avant per retener aissi cum dighs es desobre, tots hom o tota femna que sia parents o parenta del vendedor, en qualque manera sia sos parents o sa parenta, o pot retener per meissa manera cum torners, [f. 68v] si n'i agues, que s'en traisses avant tant be cum si era de son dregh torn, denant senhor e denant autrui, per tant quant autre i daria, o dat i auria; e faria meissas pagas lo torners o ·l parents cum auria estat enpres entre ·l vendedor e ·l comprador. Salb que en conquestas de heretats o d'onors no a hom torn negu per retener denant autrui aissi cum predighs es, si no era estat devas linhatge daquel o d'aquela qui vendre o volria, o d'aquel o d'aquela que per torn retener o volria.

seized on his fief, without the permission of the lord of the fief, unless he did so offering security to follow the verdict of the court. And any fief that is soldmust be sold via the possession of [*en ma de*] the lord of the fief, and that lord must receive his sales tax [*capsols*], that is to say one denier for each twelve deniers {of the sale price}, and his relief, without the lord of the fief's being able to ask for anything for handing over the fief, except his sales tax and his relief [f. 67r] alone. And he should hand over {the fief} to the buyer without further delay. Except that if the said lord wants to keep {the fief} he can do so by right of lordship in preference to an–other, for as much as the other person is willing to pay, and he can have 8 days [*dias continuables*] to take counsel, if he wants it and asks for it. And if on the due date he wants to take it, he must take it for as much as the other person is willing to pay, and make these payments immediately or on some due date, as the buyer had agreed with the seller. But if there were a remainderman [*torner*] who came forward who wanted it for his own use, that remainderman should get it in preference to the lord or anyone else, for as much as the other person would pay for it, or had paid for it. But if the lord wants to keep it, as was said above, he must swear {an oath} on the [f. 67v] Holy Gospels if the seller or the buyer requests it, that he is keeping it for his workshop [*taula*][45] or keeping it for himself with no other ruse [*genh*] and no other hidden {purpose} and without an agreement he had made to leave it to someone else, and that he will hold it for a year and a month continuously for his own purposes. But if a remainderman keeps it, as he can in preference to the lord or another person, he can sell it when he has kept it, and he can do what he wants with it whenever he wants, provided that he swears {an oath} on the Holy Gospels that when he kept it he bought it for his own personal use, without any evil ruse, and without keeping it for some other person, and without using any evil ruse. And if at the end of the above mentioned 8 days the lord of the fief does not want to keep {the fief} [f. 68r] he must immediately hand it over to the buyer at the said time, without any further delay, and with the sales tax he was to get and his relief as was said before and no more. And if he would not hand it over to the buyer as was said above, the fiefholder, that is the buyer or the seller whichever wants to do so, should complain to the council of Agen. And if he will not hand it over through {the action of} the council, {the com–plainant} can complain to the lord without any attempt at settlement. And if a remainderman, that is a man or woman who was of the kin group that had possessed the fief, does not step forward to claim the fief as was said above, any man or woman who is kin to the seller, what ever the kind of kinship, can claim in the same manner as a remainderman, [f. 68v] if there had been one who steppedforward, just as if he were a rightful remainderman, in precedence to the lord or anyone else, for the same price as {the buyer} would give or would have given, and the remainderman or the kinsman {or kinswoman} would make the same payments as had been agreed between the seller and the buyer . Except that in non-inherited property [*conquestas de heretats*] or real property given in dowry [*onor*] there is no remainderman to redeem in precedence to another, as was said above, unless it had belonged to the kin group of the man or woman who wanted to sell it, or the man or woman who wanted to redeem it as a remainderman.

[CHAPTER XXXIX]

Aissi parla dels penhs que hom fa en ma de senhor de feus, cum deu estre, ni cum lo senher o deu autrejar, ni quals dreghs i a. [f. 69r]

Tot feus que hom volha enpenhar en ma del senhor del feus, lo meiss senher lo deu autrejar de part senhoria salva sa senhoria. So es a ssaber qu'en auria sos capsols al cap de .ii. ans per tant quant seria enpenhats si empres era, si endimeghs no era souts; mas si dints los .ii. ans era souts non deu re aver, e re plus demandar non deu. E si i metia contrast no-degudament e senes razo que autrejar no o volgues, pot s'en rancurar aquel a cui ops sera al cosselh d'Agen, e si per lo cosselh autrejar no o vol pot s'en clamar al senhor senes enquesta. E si per lo meiss deute per lo qual lo feus seria enpenhats cove- [f. 69v] -nia aquel feus vendre, non deu lo senher del feus re aver plus mas aquels meiss capsols qu'en auria aguts, o deuria aver, si aguts no ·ls avia, per razo del meiss penhs, salb que si plus n'avia hom que no seria mes en penhs, d'aquo maiss auria sos capsols; mas si apres lo penhs sout aquel feus era venduts per als no pas propriament per aquel meiss deute per lo qual seria enpenhats, lo senher del feus n'auria derrescaps sos capsols tant ben cum si era venduts en simpla venda. [f. 70r]

[CHAPTER XL]

Aissi parla si ·l senher del feus autreiava ad autrui enpenhs feus que en sa ma fos a .i. enpenhat, qual pena ne deu portar.

Si alcus senher de feus autrejava feus que mogues de lui enpenhs ad autrui, esters aquel a cui primerament enpenhs l'avia autrejat, estant lo primer penhs, deu e es tenguts redre ad aquel a cui primerament l'auria autrejat tant quant lo feus valria menhs d'ambedos los deutes, senes tot perlongament, e ·l primers deutes deu estre pagats primerament avant que l'autre.

[CHAPTER XLI]

Aissi parla dels plaghs que devo estre denant senhor de feus, cum devo anar, e quals dreghs lo senher del feus i a. [f. 70v]

De tot plaghs que sia denant senhor d'alcu feus per razo de son feus dont aia agut clam deu aver lo defendeires tots sos dias costumables de cosselh, e de resposta, e de razonador, e de productio de testimonis, segont la costuma d'Agen aissi cum es dighs la ont parla sobre aitals cas dels autres plaghs qui devo venir denant lo balle del principal senhor. E del vencut deu aver lo senher d'aquel feus .v. sols de gatge, e .v.

[CHAPTER XXXIX]

Here it tells of the security deposits [*penhs*] that are made into the hands of the lord of the fief, what should happen, and how the lord should permit it, and what rights he has. [f. 69r]

{When there is} any fief that someone wants to have seized as security [*empenhar*] into the hands of the lord of the fief, the said lord should permit it, as the one holding lordship [*depart senhoria ?*] and preserving his lordship rights. That is to say that he would receive his sales tax at the end of two years for as much as had been deposited as security, if it had been seized [*si empres era*],[46] provided that it had not been paid off [*souts*]; but if within the two years it was released, he receives nothing, and may not sue for anything more. And if without a reason {the lord of he fief} raised an improper objection, {saying} that he would not permit it, the person needing to do so could complain to the council of Agen. And if {the lord of the fief} will not permit it {on the orders of} the council, {the person requesting the seizure} can complain to the{sovereign} lord without an attempt to settle [*enquesta*]. And if the said fief had to be sold because of the said debt because of which the fief was seized as security, [f. 69v] the lord of the fief should get only that same sales tax that he had received or would have received if were it not for that seizure, except that if more was held than had been given as security, he would get his sales tax for that extra; but if the fief was sold, for some other reason, after the property had been released, not precisely to pay off the debt because of which it had been deposted as a security, thelord of the fief would once again get his sales tax just as if it had been sold in an ordinary sale. [f 70r]

[CHAPTER XL]

Here it tells what fine a lord of a fief should get if he pledged to someone as a pledge an already pledged fief held from him and in his possession.

If some lord of a fief pledged an already pledged fief that was held from him to someone other than the person to whom he had previously pledged it, while the first secured debt was still outstanding, he must and he is obligated to give to the first person he pledged it to as much as the fief was less in worth than the sum of the two debts, without any delay; and the first debt must be paid off before the second.

[CHAPTER XLI]

Here it tells of the suits that should be brought before the lord of a fief, how they should be prosecuted and what fines the lord of the fief gets. [f. 70v]

In all suits before the lord of any fief, over which he has jurisdiction by reason of his fief, the defendant must have all his customary delays [*dias*] for counsel and answer and to find an advocate [*razonador*] and for the production of witnesses, according to the custom of Agen as was said where it spoke of cases in other suits that should come on before the *balle* of the sovereign lord. And the lord of that fief

sols de son feuzater defalhit, e .v. sols de sagrament jutgat en sa cort sobre alcu definiment de plag per son clam, si aquel a cui lo sagraments seria jutgats far no l' [f. 71r] auzava. E si lo senher del feus fazia demanda a son feuzater, so es a ssaber que disses que ·l feuzaters lo degues sas oblias que no l'avia pagadas sa en reire, aquel feuzaters ne deu estre creuts per son sagrament, de quants que ans aquel senher disses que ·l feuzaters lo degues sas oblias, si lo feuzaters auza jurar sobre ·ls sants evangelis que continuablement l'a pagadas sas oblias; e outra son sagrament no ·l deu anar lo senher del feus. Pero si lo feuzaters l'en cre re que no l'agues pagat de sas oblias a dia, deu lo ades pagar tant cum l'en creira, e ·l senhor del feus a sobre lui .v. sols de gatge per cadau de tants ans cum lo feuzaters lo creiria que no l'auria pagat sas oblias, e pot s'en lo senher tornar en son [f. 71v] feus, si pagar no ·l volia. E si plaghs era entre senhor de feus e son feuzater, o entre ·l feuzater e ·l senhor, de re de son feus, e sagrament era jutgats al senhor del feus que fes a son feuzater, e ·l feuzaters lo pren del senhor, lo meiss senher a sobre lui .v. sols de gatge, e son plaghs attenhns, e sas messios razonablas que auria faghs per aquel plaghs a esgart de sa cort. E si ·l feuzaters vencia lo senhor del feus lo senher no l'es tenguts desfar neguna messio que ·l feuzaters agues facha per aquel plaghs. E si plaghs o contrast era entre ·l senhor de feus e son feuzaters, so es a ssaber que ·l feuzaters lo negues son feus tot o partida, e ·l senher proava ab testimonis aondos, o ab cartas publicas, [f. 72r] que ·l feuzaters tengues de lui aquel feus, lo senher del feus auria sobre lui .v. sols de gatge per lo nec, e .v. sols de gatge de cada an de tants ans cum auria estat que no l'auria sas oblias pagadas, e totas sas oblias que ·l redria aqui meiss lo feuzaters de tants ans cum pagadas no las i auria, e sas messios razonablas que ·l deffaria a esgart de sa cort. Pero si lo senher del feus dizia que ·l feuzaters tenia mais feus de lui e ·l feuzater lo negava que no ·n tenia mas tant quant mostrat lo n'avia de lui, e ·l senher proar no o vol o no pot, e aquel feuzaters ausa jurar sobre ·ls sants evangelis que tot lo feus que el te de lui l'a mostrat, lo senher del feus no l'en pot plus demandar. E tots feuzaters pot apelar de [f. 72v] tot grevament del senhor del feus al cosselh d'Agen, aissi cum dighs es desobre de las apellacios del senhor principal. E si alcus feuzaters no servia a son senhor del feus lo feus que tenria de lui, que no ·l en pagues sas oblias, ne sos acaptes, ni sos autres devers tals cum los auria sobre ·l feus, pot s'en clamar lo senher d'aquel feus al senhor principal, son feuzater primerament enqueregut, e deu lo pagar aquel feuzaters sas oblias, e sos acaptes, e sos autres devers, e pot lo laissar lo feus servit si ·s vol lo feuzaters. E issament tots feuzaters pot laissar a son senhor lo feus que tenra de lui si se vol lo feuzaters, ab que li laisse servit e que l'en pague sas oblias, e sos acaptes, e sos autres devers. [f. 73r]

[CHAPTER XLII]

Aissi parla en qual loc li plaghs que seran denant qualsque senhors, dels quals hom tenga feus a la costuma de la ciutat d'Agen e de las gleias d'Agen, devo estre plageat.

must get 5 sous as a fine from the loser, and 5 sous from a defaulting fiefholder and 5 sous for a verdict of an oath sworn in his court in any hearing of a suit in his jurisdiction if the person who was judged to have to swear the oath did not dare to [f. 71r] swear And if the lord of the fief sued his fiefholder, that is if he said the fief–holder owed him his quit-rent that he had not paid him in the past, that fiefholder should be believed on his oath for as many years as that lord said that the fiefholder owed him his quit-rent, if the fiefholder dares to swear on the Holy Gospels that he has regularly paid him his quit-rent. And the lord of the fief should not proceed {appeal} beyond the oath. But if the fiefholder admits that he had not paid his quit-rent on the due date, he must immediately pay him as much as he admits to, and the lord of the fief gets from him 5 sous as a fine for each year he admits to not having paid him his quit-rent. And the lord can come back into his [f. 71v] fief if {the fief-holder} will not pay him. And if there was a suit between the lord of a fief and his fiefholder [*feuzater*], or between a fiefholder and the lord of the fief, concerning the fief, and the judgment was given that the lord could swear an {exculpatory} oath to his fiefholder, and the fiefholder accepted it from the lord, the said lord gets 5 sous as a fine from him, and the suit is extinguished, and {the lord} gets the reasonable costs that he incurred in that suit paid at the estimate of the court. And if the fiefholder defeated the lord of the fief, the lord is not required to reimburse [*desfar*] any costs the fiefholder incurred in that suit. And if there were a suit or quarrel between the lord of a fief and his fiefholder, that is to say if the fiefholder denied holding from him all or part of his fief, and the lord proved with numerous witnesses and public instruments [f. 72r] that the fiefholder was holding that fief from him, the lord of the fief gets 5 sous as a fine for the denial, and 5 sous per year for each year he had not paid his quit-rent, and all the {unpaid} quit-rents, paid right away, for all the years he had not been paying them, and all {the lord's} expenses that he would reimburse at the estimate of the court. But if the lord said that the fiefholder held more fiefs from him, and the fiefholder denied it, {saying} he wasn't holding any more than he had shown as holding from him, and the lord would not or could not prove {his contention}, and this fiefholder dared to swear on the Holy Gospels that he had shown him all the land he held from him, then the lord of the fief could not ask him for anything more. And any fiefholder can sue [f. 72v] before the council of Agen for any wrongdoing [*grevament*] by the lord of the fief, as is said above concerning appeals to the principal lord. And if some fiefholder did not perform the service to the lord of his fief for the fief he held from him, {that is} that he has not paid his quit-rent or his relief or his other dues whatever they were on the fief, the lord can appeal to the sovereign lord, once he has made an offer of settlement to his fiefholder, and the said fiefholder must pay his quit-rent or his relief and his other dues. And the fiefholder can abandon his paid-up [*servit*] fief to him if he wishes. And similarly any fiefholder can if he wishes abandon to his lord the fief he holds from him, provided it is paid up, andthat he pays him his quit-rent and his relief and his other dues. [f. 73r]

[CHAPTER XLII]

Here it tells of where the suits should be prosecuted that are {brought} before whatever lords fiefs are held from according to the custom of Agen and the churches [*gleias*] of Agen.

Tots plaghs que sia denant alcu senhor de feus, de negu feus que hom tenga de lui a la costuma d'Agen o de las gleias d'Agen, deu estre plageats e defenits a Agen, e la corts del senhor del feus deu estre dels proshomes d'Agen; e negus feuzaters no deu presentar dreghs de plaghs que sia de feus que tenga d'alcu senhor en autra ma, salb en la ma del senhor d'aquel feus; e si o fazia a lo senher d'aquel feus .v. sols de gatge sobre [f. 73v] lui, si aquel plaghs es entre·l senhor e·l feuzater o entre lo feuzater e·l senhor. E si alcus senher de feus a clamant de son feuzater de feus que tenga de lui, lo feuzaters deu far dreghs en la ma d'aquel senhor de cui tenra aquel feus; e si lo feuzaters no vol far dreghs en la ma del senhor d'aquel feus, lo senher d'aquel feus l'en deu destrenher el meiss feus. E si alcus hom fa demanda ad autre de feus que tenga de senhor en alcuna cort, qualsque sia la corts, e aquel feuzaters lo presenta dregh en la ma del senhor de cui o te feuzalment, no l'es tenguts seguir plagear en neguna cort mas solament denant lo senhor de cui o te feuzalment; pero mentaure deu en la cort lo senhor de cui dira que te aquel feus. [f. 74r]

[CHAPTER XLIII]

Aissi parla d'ome si muria senes orde, e heret no avia, que deu estre faghs de sas causas.

Si alcus hom muria a Agen senes orde o senes heret que no agues, lo cosselhs d'Agen deu prendre en garda totas las causas d'aquel mort, moblas e no-moblas, e deu las tener .i. an e .i. mes. E si dints aquel an e aquel mes se traia avant parents o parenta del mort, aquel o aquela cobraria totas las causas d'aquel mort, proat aondozament lo parentat; e si dints lo meiss terme no era [f. 74v] venguts avant parents o parenta d'aquel mort que proes sufficientment lo parentat, lo feus del mort si n'avia tornaria ad aquel senhor de cui lo tenria feuzalment, e las causas moblas al senhor principal de la terra. Mas pero qual que hora i vengues, parents o parenta del mort deu cobrar totas las causas d'aquel son parent mort, soutament senes tot contrast, proat suficientment lo parentat.

[CHAPTER XLIV]

Aissi parla dels sobreafeuzaments, en qual manera hom los pot far.

Si alcus hom vol sobreafeuzar feus que tenga a la costuma d'Agen, pot o far, ab que si retenga capfeus, ab que [f. 75r] l'uzatges que issira d'aquel capfeus pusca valer cada ant tant cum las oblias del meiss feus seran cada an. E·l primers senher de cui hom tenra aquela terra o aquel feus sobrefeuzat o sobrefeuzada deu ne aver los primers capsols, e pot s'en tornar lo primer senher el meiss feus per sos capsols si hom no·ls i paga. E si aquel qui sobreafeuzara no si rete capfeus valent, aissi

Any suit that is brought before some lord of a fief concerning a fief held from him according to the custom of Agen or of the *gleias* of Agen, must be pleaded and concluded in Agen, and the court of the lord of the fief must be composed of good-men of Agen. And no fiefholder shall present a suit concerning a fief he holds from some lord to the adjudication of any person [*en autra ma*] except the lord of that fief, and if he did the lord of that fief would get 5 sous as a fine from [f. 73v] him, if the suit is between lord and fiefholder or between fiefholder and lord. And if some lord of a fief has a complaint from his fiefholder concerning the fief he holds from him, the fiefholder must give jurisdiction [*far dregs en la ma de...*][47] to the lord from whom he holds the fief. And if the fiefholder will not give jurisdiction to the lord of that fief, the lord of the fief must distrain him {by seizing some property} on that fief. And if some man brings a complaint in some court, whatever court it is, against another man concerning a fief he holds from a lord, and the fiefholder gives juris–diction[48] to the lord from whom he holds his court feudally, he is not required to plead in any other court except only before the lord from whom he holds {the fief} feudally. But he must inform the {other} court {of the name of} the lord from whom he claims to hold that fief. [f. 74r]

[CHAPTER XLIII]

Here it tells of what should be done with a man's property if he died without a will [*orde*] and he had no heir.

If a man dies in Agen without a will and without an heir, the council of Agen should take all the property of that dead man into its custody, real and personal property, and should keep it for a year and a month. And if within that year and month a male or female relative of that dead man comes forward, that person would recover all the property of that dead person, once the kinship had been abundantly proved. And if in the same period no [f. 74v] male or female relative of that dead person had come forward who was able to prove the kinship sufficiently, the fief of the deceased, if he had one, would go back to the lord from whom he had held it feudally, and the personal property would go to the sovereign lord of the district. However, at whatever moment there came a male or female relative of the deceased, he or she should recover all the property of their dead relative, freely, without any dispute, once the kinship was adequately proved.

[CHAPTER XLIV]

Here it speaks of subinfeudations and how you can create them.

If some man wants to subinfeudate a fief that he holds according to the custom of Agen, he can do so provided that he retains a domainal portion [*capfeus*], such that [f. 75r] the funds [*uzatges*] that are derived from this domainal portion are worth as much each year as the quit-rent [*oblias*] of the same fief is each year. And the overlord [*primers senhor*] from whom that subinfeudated land or fief is held must receive the first sales tax [*capsols*], and if it is not paid to him the first lord can go on to the fief to

cum predighs es, totas las oblias degudas per aquel sobreafeuzament e ·l meiss feus sobreafeuzats tornaria al primer senhor. So es a ssaber en aital manera que li feuzater als quals hom o auria sobreafeuzat lo pagario cada an totas las oblias qu'en deurio far, e tenrio lo feus de lui per las partidas que cadaus ne tenria; pero si ·l feuzaters en aquel sobre–afeu- [f. 75v] -zament no se avia retengudas tantas oblias cum las primeras serio, li feuzater qui aquel feus sobreafeuzat tenrio devo complir al primer senhor tant quant menhs ne seria, cadaus per razo que cadaus tenria del feus. E si lo sobreafeuzaires se dezissia del capfeus, totas las oblias tornario al primer senhor, so es a ssaber que li feuzater las i fario cada an, e tenrio lo feus de lui cadaus per sa partida, si aquel qui o auria sobreafeuzat ab sa volontat dezissiz no s'en era. ¶Item: lo sobreafeuzaires no pot dar, ni vendre, ni alienar en neguna manera lo capfeus que se retenra, si de tot lo feus no ·s dezissia; ni ·l pot logar ni prestar mas solament a terme saubut, e aquo a terme [f. 76r] de .x. ans al plus lonh, o d'aqui en jus, a cada vets que logar o prestar lo volra; e si o fazia en autra manera que dighs es desobre, lo meiss capfeus e totas las oblias que ·l so–brefeuzaires si auria retengudas tornario al primer senhor del feus, so es a ssaber en aital manera que li feuzater que i serio per aquel sobreafeuzament serio assout del sobre–feuzador, e tenrio tot lo feus del primer senhor de cui lo sob[r]e– feuzaires o tenria, e redrio tots temps las oblias qu'en fario al sobrefeuzador. Salb empero que tots hom o tota femna que aia agut ni tengut en bona possessio, el o aquel o aquilh per cui i sera, oblias o feus alcu senes capfeus, .xxx. ans o plus, d'aqui en la es prescriut contra ·l senhor del feus, [f. 76v] e contra tota autra persona, que re no li pot hom d'aqui en la demandar. ¶Item: si ·l senher del feus demanda a son feuzater carta de reconoissensa del feus que tenra de lui, e que l'assigne son capfeus en loc cert del meiss feus si sobreafeuzat i a, lo feuzaters o deu far senes tot contrast, e senes tot plaghs que no i pot metre. E per meissa manera lo senher del feus deu dar a son feuzater, si o requer, carta de reconoissensa e de reves–timent del feus, que tenra de lui sa senhoria salva. E negus feuzaters no pot ni deu far teulera ni peireira per vendre en feus que tenga d'autrui, senes volontat del senhor del feus. ¶Item: tots homquals que sia, clercs o laics, que tenga o heretat [f. 77r] a la cos–tuma d'Agen deu dar per liuras a las messios comunals de la meissa ciutat. ¶Item: si alcus se clamava al senhor, so es al balle de la senhoria principal, de re que tengues feuzalment d'autrui, so es a ssaber sobre la proprietat o que toques la proprietat, lui presentant dreghs denant lo senhor del feus, deu lo gitar de la ma del senhor, si per falha o per negligentia del senhor del feus, que dreghs no l'en fes segont los dias costumables d'Agen, clamats no s'en era.

get his sales tax. And if the person subinfeudating does not keep a domainal portion [*capfeus*] worth, as was stated above, as much as all the quit-rent owed for the subinfeudated land, the said subinfeudated fief would go back to the overlord. That is to say in such a way that the fiefholders to whom the subinfeudation had been made would pay to him each year all the quit-rent that they owed, and would hold the fief from him according to the share that each one took. But if the fiefholder in that subinfeudation [f. 75v] had not retained as much in quit-rent as the original quit-rent due to the overlord would be, then the fiefholders who held the subinfeudated fiefs would have to make up the deficit to the overlord, each one in proportion to what he held of the fief. And if the man making the subinfeudation gave up his seisin of the domainal portion, all the quit-rent would go back to the overlord, that is to say, that the fiefholders would pay it each year, and each would hold their shares in the fief from him, if the person making the subinfeudation had not {already} given them up at his own free will. ¶Item, the person making the subinfeudation may not give or sell or alienate in any manner the domainal portion that he keeps, unless he gives up seisin of the whole fief, nor can he rent it or lend it except for a fixed term, and the term must be [f. 76r] for ten years at the longest, or less than ten years, each time he wants to rent it or lend it. And if he did so in some other manner than what is des- cribed above, the said domainal portion and all the quitrent that the person making the subinfeudation had kept for himself would go back to the overlord of the fief. That is to say, in such a way that the fiefholders who were there as a result of the subinfeud- ation would be released from the person making the subinfeudation, and would hold the whole fief from the overlord from whom the person making the subinfeudation held it, and would always pay {the overlord} the quit-rent they had owed the person making the subinfeudation. Except, however, that all men and women who had had or held in good possession (he or the person or persons who had put him in possession) {the right to collect} quit-rent, or a fief without any domainal portion, for 30 years or more, {then} from then on he is secure [*prescriut*] against the lord of the fief [f. 76v] and against any other person, for from then on no one can sue him for anything. ¶Item If the lord of the fief asks his fiefholder for a written avowal {of lordship} [*carta de reconoissenssa*] for the fief he holds from him (and to designate to him his domainal portion in a certain place on the said fief, if there is a sub-fiefholder), the fiefholder must do so without any dispute and any suit. And in the same way the lord of the fief must give his fiefholder if he wants one a written acknowledgment and investment [*carta de reconoissensa e de revestiment*] in the fief which he holds from him, preserving the seignorial rights of the lord. And no fiefholder can or should make a tile factory [*teularia*] or stone quarry [*peireira*] to make sales on a fief he holds from someone else, without the permission of the lord of the fief. ¶Item any man, whether lay or cleric, who has possession or owns a fief [f. 77r] according to the custom of Agen must give proportionately [*per liuras*][49] to the communal expen- ses of the said city. ¶Item if any man makes a complaint to the lord, that is to the *balle* of the principal lordship, on any thing he holds as a fief from someone else (that is, a suit on the ownership, or touching the ownership), bringing a suit against the lord of the fief, he{the *balle*}should refuse jurisdiction [*gitar de la ma del senhor*] unless he was com–plaining that the lord of the fief had not given him a hearing according to the customary court sittings [*dias*] of Agen, out of omission or negligence.

[CHAPTER XLV]

D'una manera de possessio parla aquest capitols, de calonja quant es entre doas personas, e cadaus di que possediss la causa dont es calonja entre lor. [f. 77v]

Cum mantas vets avenga que alcu vendo, o afeuzo, o dono, o cambio, o empenho, o en autra manera aliano maio, o terra, o vinha, o autra heretat a una persona, e enapres la vendo, o la afeuzo, o la aliano, o la enpenho, ad autrui, e la us es ne mes en possessio en la ma del senhor del feus, e l'autre no, e ambedui dizo que possedisso, ad aquel qui per carta publica o per autras proansas leials proara sa possessio, so es a ssaber que aquela causa aia en ma del senhor del feus, e l'autre proa qu'en es en possessio per aquel de cui la causa era, mas no en la ma del senhor del feus, es jutgada la possessios, e no a l' [f. 78r] autre que no proa que l'aia en la ma del senhor del feus. Mas si sobre las despessas es questios, que aquel a cui sera jutgada la possessios las demande per lo plaghs qu'en sera estats, l'autra parts las i es tenguda pagar las despessas, taxadas e juradas per l'ofici del jutge, e aquel qui las despessas aura pagadas pot las demandar ad aquel qui aquela causa l'auria venduda, o enpenhada, o alianada, o afeuzada aissi cum predighs es.

[CHAPTER XLVI]

Cum soent avenga que alcu se traho denant los senhors dels feus per alcuna causa que an venduda, o volho vendre, de son feus e despoiss que denant alcu senhor d'aquel feus s'en seran presentat, aquela venda remania que no·s fes, [f. 78v] sobre aital cas parla aquest capitols, qu'en es ni qu'en deu estre faghs.

Si despoiss que·l feuzaters se sera presentats denant lo senhor de causa que fos de son feus que agues venduda ad autrui, e aquela venda remania que no·s fes entre·l vendedor e·l comprador, lo senher del feus ges per aquo non pert sas vendas, ans las deu aver entegrament, e pot ne penhorar el meiss feus. E si despoiss que aquela venda seria desfacha la meissa causa era venduda ad autrui, lo senher del feus n'auria tambe autra vets sas vendas, de tant cum aquela causa seria venduda, d'aquel qui [f. 79r] comprat o auria; mas si aquel meiss qui primerament o auria comprat o retenia despoiss que la primera venda seria desfacha, passaria ab las primeras vendas, que plus non pagaria vendas per razo d'aquelas vendicios, e pagaria las al senhor d'aquel feus, si agudas no las avia, o al vendedor si pagadas las avia. E·l senher del feus no a torn negu en causa que hom tenga de lui a feus que sia dada en donatio, pero per que la donacios sia facha a bona fe, no per barat, ni en causa escambiada una per autra, salb

[CHAPTER XLV]

This chapter tells of one kind of possession, concerning a challenge, when it occurs between two persons and each person claims {possession of} the thing that is the subject of the challenge between them. [f. 77v]

As it often occurs that someone sells or infeudates, or gives or exchanges or deposits as security [*empenho*] or in some other manner alienates a house or some other real property to a person, and then afterwards sells it or infeudates it or alienates it or deposits it as security to some another person, and one is put in possession through the lord's jurtisdiction [*en la ma del senhor*] and the other is not, and both say they are in possession, the possession is judged to go[50] to the person who proves his possession by means of a public instrument, or by other legal methods, that is to say, who obtains the property [*causa*] through the lord of the fief's jurisdiction's possession, where the other person proves he obtained the property from the person whose property it was, but not through the lord of the fief's jurisdiction, and {it will} not {go to} the [f.78r] other man who does not prove he obtained it from the lord of the fief possession. But if the issue of expenses is raised, if the party to whom the possession is awarded asks for expenses for the suit that was brought concerning {the possession}, the other party is required to pay expenses, assessed and sworn by the judge in his official capacity. And the person who has paid expenses can sue for them from the person who sold or deposited as security or alienated or infeudated the property to him as was said above.

[CHAPTER XLVI]

As if often happens that someone appears before the lords of the fief because of some property they have sold or want to sell belonging to the fief, and when they have appeared before the lord of that fief the sale is cancelled and does not take place, [f. 78v] this chapter tells of that situation, concerning what is done and what should be done.

If after the fiefholder has appeared before the lord concerning his fief which he has sold to someone else, and the sale has been cancelled so that it does not take place between the seller and the buyer, the lord of the fief does not on that account lose his sales tax [*uendas*], indeed he gets it in its entirety, and he can seize property [*penhorar*] as security} on the said fief. And if after the sale was nullified the same property was sold to someone else, the lord of the fief would nevertheless get his full sales tax over again for as much as the property was sold for, from the [f. 79r] person who had bought it. But if the person who had originally bought it did buy it after the first sale had been nullified, he would have given satisfaction [*passaria*] with the first sales tax, and would not pay sales tax because of the {second} purchase, and would pay it to the {over}lord of that fief if he had not received it or to the vendor if *he* had paid it. And the lord of the fief has no remainder [*torn*] in property that is held from him as a fief that is given as a gift, provided the gift is given in good faith, and not in fraud, nor as an exchange of property one thing for another. Except that if there was

que si i avia diners dats o promes per tornas, d'aquelas tornas auria lo senher a cui lo dreghs d'aquelas tornas venria sas vendas, segont que i auria diners dats o promes. [f. 79v]

[CHAPTER XLVII]

De contrast si avenia entre alcunas personas sobre feus conjonts que se toquo, e movo de dos senhors, o de pluzors, cum se deu deffenir aquel contrast, parla aquest capitols.

Si contrast o plags era entre alcus sobre feus conjonts que se toquo, que movo de dos senhors o de pluzors, aquelh senhor i devo establir cort comunal, la quals corts aquel contrast o aquel plaghs diffinisca per los dias costumables, senes autres no-deguts alongaments; o si aquilh senhor, o alcus de lor, o lor corts, ne ero deffalhents, o negligent, ni i metio no-deguts alongaments; o si aquilh senhor, o alcus de lor, o lor corts, ne ero deffalhents, o negligent, ni i metio no-deguts alongaments outra los [f. 80r] dias acostumables, la parts que ·l tort prendria s'en pot clamar al senhor major o a son balle per sa propria auctoritat.

[CHAPTER XLVIII]

Conseguentre digam si alcus feuzaters era rebelles, que no volgues estar a dreghs denant lo senhor del feus de demanda que hom lo fes en causa que tengues de lui a feus, o sos dreghs redre no ·l volia, qu'en deu estre faghs.

Si alcus feuzaters era rebelles, que no volgues estar a dreghs denant lo senhor del feus de demanda que hom lo fes en re que tengues de lui a feus, o sas drechuras redre no ·l volia, per lui ni per penhora, ni per als, lo [f. 80v] senher d'aquel feus pot prendre dels frughs que i trobara per far sas volontats, senes que ·ls frughs qu'en prendra no devo caer en souta, ni en paga de sos dreghs, so es a entendre agras, o vendenha de vinhas, o frughs d'arbles o d'autra causa plantada o semnada en vinhas, o en terras, o de blats, o d'arbles de terra o de boscs, o ortalezia de casal, o peiss de pescaria. Mas pero tantost cum aquel feuzaters venria al senhor d'aquel feus per far son dever, lo senher se deu laissar d'aqui en la de prendre aquels frugs, ni ·l senher del feus no ·s pot tornar en re als que ·l feuzaters aia, salb en aquo que de lui tenra tant solament a feus, ni ad autrui clamar no s'en pot. Mas lo senher del [f. 81r] feus pot penhorar son feuzater el feus que de lui tenra per sos dreghs, o per clam d'autrui qui sobre ·l meiss feus se clamaria a lui, si ·l feuzaters era defalhents de far dreghs denant lui o de pagar sos gatges, senes que non es tenguts al principal senhor ni ad autrui.

money given or promised in addition [*tornas*],[51] the lord to whom the rights of the addition [*tornas*] came would have sales tax on the addition, according to what money was given or promised. [f. 79v]

[CHAPTER XLVII]

This chapter tells how a disagreement should be brought to a conclusion, if it should come about between various persons concerning adjoining fiefs that abut each other, and that are held [*mavo* for *movo*][52] from two or several lords,.

If there were a disagreement or suit between several persons concerning adjoining fiefs that abut each other and that are held from two or more lords, these lords should establish a common court, which should bring that disagreement or suit to a conclusion in the customary period [*dias costumables*], without any other undue delay; or if these lords or any of them or their courts were in default or negligent or imposed undue delays beyond [f. 80r] the customary period, the party suffering the wrong could make a complaint to the overlord [*senhor maior*] or his *balle* on his own authority.

CHAPTER XLVIII]

Continuing, we tell what should be done if some fiefholder was rebellious, so that he did not want to appear in court before the lord of his fief concerning a complaint made against him by someone concerning some property he held from him as a fief, or did not want to give him his dues [*sos dreghs redre*].

If some fiefholder was rebellious so that he did not want to appear in court before the lord of the fief concerning a claim by some man concerning some property he held from him as a fief, or who would not give him a hearing [*sas drechuras redre*] whether by personal intervention [*per lui*] or by seizure of property [*penhora*] or by anything else, [f. 80v] then the lord of that fief can take the fruits he finds there, to do what he wants with, without those fruits he takes being counted as satisfaction of payment in his suit or as a fine [*en paga de sos dreghs*]. That is to say fields [*agras*], or the harvest from vines, or the fruits of trees or other things planted or sown in vineyards or fields, whether wheat, or trees from fields or woods, or produce from gardens or fish from fishponds. But as soon as that fiefholder came to the lord to do his duty, the lord should desist from taking these fruits from then on. And the lord of the fief cannot have recourse to anything else that the fiefholder has, but only to what he holds from him as a fief, and he cannot make a complaint to anyone else. But the lord of [Folio 81 recto] the fief can seize property from his fiefholder and the fief he holds from him for his fine [*sos dreghs*] or for the complaint of another person if the fiefholder defaulted on an appearance before him, or for payment of his fines, without being answerable to the principal lord or to anyone else.

[CHAPTER XLIX]

Aquest capitols parla del fachs comunal de la notaria d'Agen.

E es a ssaber que lo cosselhs e la universitaz d'Agen, o la una partida per lor e per tota la universitat, crean e fan e pauzan notaris en la ciutat d'Agen, e ·ls podo far e metre e pauzar e [f. 81v] donar plenera auctoritat de far generalment e universalment cartas, instruments, notas, prothocols, actas escriure, testimonis exeminar, e publicar aquels, e far totas e senglas autras causas per tots los locs e ensengles on ne serion requeregut; e aquesta costuma a estat obtenguda e autrejada per los senhors al dichs cosselh e a la universitat continuadament e ses tot meja del temps en sa que primerament foro fachs, e creat, e pauzat a Agen ni en lo ebescat d'Agenes. E li notari devo estre francs de questa e d'ost de vila, la qual franquessa an e devo aver, car cada notaris e tuchs ensems devo venir al man- [f. 82r] -dament del cosselh, e devo far los escriutz necessaris e covinals al cosselh e a la universitat, e devo anar dins e defora per los propris negocis del cosselh e de la universitat, a la messio de la vila ses tot pretz, e devo far generalment e especialment segont la bona ordinatio del cosselh aquels negocis que seran necessaris al cosselh e a la universitat sobredichs. E que nulha persona no sia receubuda en notari si no sabia far cartas en romans e en latii, e que fos covenabla persona e de leial matrimoni en leialtat e en autras causas.

[CHAPTER L]

Aquest capitols parla dels devers que li notari d'Agen devo aver e prendre de las cartas, qualsque [f. 82v] las cartas sio que hom fa enquerre a lor e tornar em publica forma.

E es a ssaber de carta simpla de deute .ii. deners; de carta de deute ab sagrament .ii. diners; de carta ab ostadge ses sagrament .iiii. diners. ¶De carta de deute en que aia ostadge e sagrament .vi. diners. ¶De carta de penhs cimpla .iiii. diners. ¶De carta de penhs on aia mester sagrament o renunciament de molher, o renuntiament de dot, o d'enfant que sia mendre d'etat .xii. diners. ¶De carta de la tenor sobredicha don cove anar denant l'official .ii. sols. [f. 83r] ¶De carta de companhia partida per .a. b. c .xii. deners de cadauna. ¶De carta de companhia d'una tenor .xii. deners de cadauna. ¶De carta de reconoissansa de paga facha .ii. diners. ¶De carta que balla buou o autre bestiar en companhia .iiii. deners. ¶De carta de fret .iiii. deners. ¶De carta quant hom promet autre gardar de dan quant l'a mes en fermansa o que l'aia mes cabaler .ii. diners. ¶De carta de loguer de maios .iiii. diners, e tota carta que sia facha en esta vila d'ome estranh, que l'escrivas non prenga mas cum faria de borgues de la vila, e si

[CHAPTER XLIX}

This chapter speaks of the public activity of the Agen notariate.

And it should be known that the council and the whole community of Agen or a part of it for them and for the whole community create and make and appoint nota- ries in the city of Agen and they can create and make and appoint them and [f. 81v] give them, generally and universally, full authority to create documents [*cartas*],[53] instruments [*instruments*], notes, protocols, to write acts, to examine wills and publish the same, and to do each and every other thing in each and every place where they are asked to do so, and this custom was obtained from and authorized by the lords to the said council and to the whole community in perpetuity [*continuadament*] and without any lapse [*meia*] of time since they were first made and created and appointed in Agen and in the diocese of Agen. And the notaries must be exempt from the city taxes [*questa*] and the mobilization [*ost*] of the town. They have and must have this exemption, for each and all notaries must appear on the com- [f. 82r] -mand of the council, and write the necessary and public [*covinal*][54] writings of the council and the whole community, and they must travel within and without {the city} on the business of the council and the whole community at the expense of the city without any remu- neration [*ses tot pretz*] and must conduct generally and in particular, according to the proper [*bona*] orders of the council, the business that is necessary for the aforesaid council and whole community. And no person may be appointed a notary unless he can write instruments in romance {Occitan} and in Latin, and is a proper person and {born of a} legal marriage, and in regard to his honesty and other things.

CHAPTER L]

This chapter speaks of the fees that the notaries of Agen must get and charge for the instruments, whatever kind [f. 82v] they are that they are asked to write and draw up in official form [*tornar en publica forma*].

Let it be known, that for a simple instrument on debt [*carta simpla de deute*], {the charge is} 2 deniers; for an instrument on debt with an oath, 2 deniers; for an instrument with a surety [*ostadge*] without an oath 4 deniers; ¶ For an instrument on debt in which there is a surety and an oath, 6 deniers; For a simple instrument for security [*penhs*] 4 deniers; for an instrument of security where there is needed an oath or the renunciation by a wife or the renunciation of a dowry, or by a child under age, 12 deniers; ¶For an instrument on the same matter as above where an appearance be- fore the ecclesiastical judge [*official*] is required, 2 sous; [f. 83r] For an instrument of a partnership divided a,b,c, 12 deniers each {party}; for an instrument of partnership in duplicate, 12 deniers each; for an instrument of acknowledgment of a debt paid, 2 deniers; ¶ For an instrument that gives an ox or other livestock in partnership, 4 deniers; ¶ For an instrument of transportation 4 deniers; ¶ For an instrument when a man promises to keep another man harmless when he has named him as surety or has made him a knight 2 deniers; ¶For instrument on a house rental, 4 deniers and for any instrument made in this city for a foreigner the redactor may not charge more than

grans fachs de cartas d'omes estranhs com a de baros, o [f. 83v] de cavalers, o de clercs que ilh n'aion a la conoguda del cosselh. ¶De carta de covens quant se dona per esta dia a temps .vi. diners, ab sagrament o ses sagrament. ¶De carta de compromes d'arbitres .ii. sols ab sagrament, o ses sagrament, o ab fermansas. ¶De carta de covents d'obra far de maios .vi. diners. ¶De carta de covents quant hom vent vis a pagar en la terra .xii. diners. ¶De carta de procuratio .xii. diners. ¶De carta de tutoria .xii. diners. ¶De carta de curador .xii. diners. ¶De carta de venda de terras o d'eretas simpla .iiii. diners. ¶De carta de reconoissensa de feus .iiii. diners. ¶De car- [f. 84r] -ta de venda d'eretats on aia sagrament o renuntiament de molher o d'enfant que sia mener d'etat .xii. diners, e si causa es que l'escriva covenga anar denant l'official .ii. sols. ¶De carta d'arrendament simpla .xii. diners. ¶De carta d'arrendament de pesatges o d'eissament d'eretats .iiii. sols. ¶De carta d'escambis .xii. diners. ¶De carta de parti- zos d'eretats que la partizos valgues .c. sols .iiii. diners de cadauna, e de .xx. liuras .xii. diners, e de .m. sols .xii. diners, e d'aqui en sus entroque .d. liuras per razo.

De carta d'ordre de .m. sols .xii. diners, e de cada .m. sols entroque .d. libras per razo, [f. 84v] e de quant que sia la carta de l'ordre d'aqui en sus no·n deu plus prendre mas .x. sols. ¶De carta de maridatge partida per a. b. c. xii. diners de cadauna. ¶E que las cartas que seran enquestas devo esser notadas lo meiss dia ades en presentia de las parts el paper, e que tota la nota de la dicha carta sia pleneramente el paper contenguda, e que en aquela meissa manera sia tornada e reduda en publica forma ses tot mermament e ses tot acreissement, cum sera en la nota del paper, e no en autra manera. E si alcus hom de la vila d'Agen venia de la meissa vila de nochs o de dias, que l'agues obs per negun [f. 85r] home que fos cochadz de malaudia que volgues far ordre, l'escrivas i deu anar ab aquel que obs l'aura; e si anar no i volia, el estaria en la merse del cosselh en voluntat de perdre l'ofici de la notaria.

E que negus escrivas d'esta vila no an deforas la vila ab home estranh foras los decs, si no o faia ab voluntat del cosselh, ni no ane foras d'esta vila per razo de plags, ni per testimonis auzir, ni per razonar, ni per auzir plags per razo que fos jutges, si no o faia ab borgues d'esta vila, per razo de cartas far, ni en autra manera e si o faia estaria en la voluntat del cosselh e de la universitat de perdre l'offici de la notaria.

[CHAPTER LI]

Aquest capitols parla del fachs de batalha. [f. 85v]

So es a ssaber, que negus hom ciutadas d'Agen, ni dels borcs, ni dels apertenements no deu ni pot estre constre(n)hs per la costuma d'Agen a far batalha si

{he would} a bourgeois of this town; and in instruments for foreign men in such great matters as those of barons [f. 83v] or knights or clerks, they should be paid at the estimate of the council. ¶For an instrument of agreement when it is given from today for a set term, 6 deniers with an oath or without an oath; ¶For an instrument with an arbitration protocol, 2 sous with an oath or without an oath or with sureties. ¶For an instrument of agreement for work to be done on a house 6 deniers. ¶For an instrument of agreement when wine is sold to be paid in the district, 12 deniers. ¶For an instrument appointing an attorney 12 deniers. ¶For an instrument of custodian–ship [*tutoria*] 12 deniers. ¶For an instrument of curatorship [*curador*] 12 deniers. ¶For an instrument for the simple sale of land or real property [*eretas*] 4 deniers. ¶For an instrument of acknowledgment for a fief 4 deniers. ¶ For an instrument [f. 84r] for the sale of real property where there is an oath or the renunciation by a wife or a child who is a minor, 12 deniers, and if there is a reason why the writer must appear before the ecclesiastical judge, 2 sous. ¶ For a simple instrument of giving a rental, 12 de–niers. ¶For an instrument giving the rental of a toll-collection or an easement [*eis–sament*] of real property, 4 sous. ¶For an instrument of exchange {of property}, 12 deniers. ¶For an instrument of partition of an inheritance where the partition is worth 100 sous, 4 deniers from each party, and for 20 livres 12 deniers, and for 1000 sous 12 deniers, and from there on up to 500 livres in proportion.[55]

For a will of 1000 sous, 12 deniers and for each 1000 sous up to 500 livres in proportion, [f. 84v] and for however much the will is from there on up he should take no more than 10 sous. ¶For an instrument of marriage divided a, b, c, 12 deniers from each party. ¶And the instruments that are requested should always be written on the same day in the presence of the parties to the rough copy [*paper*], and all the writing of the said instrument should be fully contained in the rough copy, and it should thus be turned into and reduced to the official form without any reduction and without any addition, as it is in the rough copy of the paper, and not in any other manner. And if some man of the town of Agen came from the said town by night or day who was in need because of some [f. 85r] man who was laid up with sickness and who wanted to make a will, then the writer must go there with the person who needed him, and if he would not go he would risk losing his appointment of notary at the discretion of the council.

And let no writer from this town go outside the town with a foreigner outside the city limits [*decs*], unless he does so at the will of the council. Nor let him go out-side this town for a lawsuit nor to hear a witness, nor to be an advocate nor to hear a case because he is a judge – unless he does so with a bourgeois of this town in order to make an instrument – nor in any other way, (and if he did he would be in danger of losing the position of notary at the will of the council and the whole community).[56]

[CHAPTER LI]

This chapter speaks of duels [*fachs de batalha*]. [f. 85v]

Let it be known that no man who is a citizen of Agen or the suburbs or the de-

no ·s vol; e si alcuna persona l'apela de fachs de crim o de traissio e el met sas deffensios, so es a ssaber que el diga que "Eu so pros hom e leials, e no so ni vulh estre tengut ni encolpat d'aquel fachs ni d'autre semblant d'aquel, e dic que no so tengutz de batalha per la costuma d'esta vila," aqui meiss lo ciutadas o l'abitans pot desmentir aquel qui l'aura apelat d'aquela manera que ·s volra del [f 86r] dichs apel, e no es tengutz que s'en batalhe si met meja abans la desmentizo. Empero si de voluntat d'una part e d'autra s'obligavan a far batalha, e la batalha se fazia, li senhor d'Agen devo aver lo caval e las armas d'aquel que vencutz sera, e devo punir la persona vencuda, segont que ·l fachs del apel seria. Empero si abans que intresson en camp tractaments de patz avenia entre lor, e fazio patz, li senhor i an .lxv. sols en cada partida, si avant ab los senhors no era estat tractat que fesso gratia del meiss gatge, e si causa es que aquel que sera apelatz se defen- [f 86v] -da que no es tengutz de batalha per las razos sobre dichas, aqui meiss el se pot clamar al s senhors de l'aunta e de la enjuria que l'apelans l'aura dicha fazen lo dichs apel, e li senhor devo li far desfar los costs e las messios que fachas n'aura la persona apelada d'avocadz, e d'escriuts, e d'autras causas, e de la enjuria deu li far emenda la persona apelants tant quant la persona apelada auzara jurar que per aitant no o volgra aissi estre apeladz ne fachs lo dichs apel, ni dicha la injuria ni facha; pero primerament apres aisso facha taxatios per los senhors e per lo cosselh ensems, segont dr(e)chs. [f. 87r]

[CHAPTER LII]

Aquest capitols parla d'aquelas personas de las quals lo cosselh d'Agen deu enlegir l'autre cosselh que s'ensegua apres de la ciutat e dels borcs d'Agen.

E es a ssaber que lo cosselhs, la on electio se fara del cosselh autre apres, aissi cum se muda l'aus apres l'autre, devo enlegir prohomes, e leials, e catholics, e tals que no sian infam, e que sian de leial matrimoni, e que no sian heretge, ni ensabatat, ni filh ni fraire de heretge ni neguna persona que sia estatz condempnatz del fachs de la heretgia, ne sia estatz [Folio 87 verso] crozatz ni emuratz del meiss fachs, ni que sia usurers manifestz, ni estatz vencuz de lachs crim, aissi cum es de corre vila e de pujar en espillori.

Lo cosselh d'Agen deu e pot traire, per sa propria auctoritat, lan que sera cosselh de la universitat, de la ciutat, e dels borcs, e de tots los borzes d'Agen, totas e senglas las messios que faran per los comunals negocis de la universitat, de la ciutat, e dels borcs d'Agen, en qualque manera messios fassan, per un escriva e per dos autres messatges que deu e pot aver lo cosselh d'Agen per las necessitats de lor e de la universitat, e per dos trompadors li qual devo far la crida e las cridas que ·s faran ab trompas per comandament del cosselh d'Agen, e no en autra manera, exceptadas [f.

pendencies should or can be forced by the custom of Agen to fight a {judicial} battle if he does not want to, and if some person accuses him of a crime or a treachery [*traissio*] and he raises his defense, that is to say that he says "I am a good and proper man [*proshom e leials*] and I am not and do not want to be incriminated or exculpated by this battle [*fachs*] or any other like it; and I say that I am not required to do battle by the custom of this town;" {and} here the citizen or inhabitant can give the lie [*desmentir*] the person who has accused him in whatever manner he wants concerning the [f. 86r] said accusation, and he is not required to do battle if he leaves an interval [*met meia ?*] before the giving of the lie [*desmentizo*]. But if both parties pledged themselves to do battle, and the battle took place, the lords of Agen must be given the horse and arms of the person defeated, and must punish the vanquished person according to the subject of the appeal. But if before they entered the field {of battle} a peace negotiation began between then and they made peace, the lords get 65 sous from each party unless there had been an agreement previously with the lords that they would forgive the said fine. And in a case where the person appealed against raises the defense [f. 86v] that he is not obliged to do battle for the reasons men–tioned above, right then he can complain to the lords about the shame and out-rage that the appellant caused him by making the said appeal, and the lords must make {the appellant} reimburse the person appealed against for his costs and ex–penses in hiring advocates and having writings made and other matters. And the person appealing must pay as much in a fine for the outrage as the person dares swear {represents his wish} not to have been appealed against, nor the said appeal lodged nor the injury said and done,[57] but with the estimate being made right after this by the lords and the council together, in a fair manner [*segont dr[e]chs*].[58] [f. 87r]

[CHAPTER LII]

This chapter speaks of the persons from among whom the council of Agen must elect the next following council of the city and suburbs of Agen.

Let it be known that when there is an election of the next council, as one follows another, the council should elect goodmen, honest [*leial*] and catholic, and such that are not of of ill repute [*infam*] and who are {born of a} legal marriage, and who are not heretics or vaudois [*ensabatat*], nor sons or brothers of heretics, nor any person who has been condemned for a heretical act, nor who has been [f. 87v] on a crusade [*crozatz*] or imprisoned [*emuratz*] for the said act, nor who is a known usurer nor convicted of an evil crime, (for example {whose punishment is} to run through the town or to mount the pillory.)[59]

The council of Agen should and can, when it is a council of the whole community of the city and the suburbs and of all the bourgeois of Agen, be reimbursed [*traire*] on its own authority for each and every expense for the public business of the whole community, the city and suburbs of Agen, however these expenses are made, for one scribe and two other messengers which the council of Agen can and should have for its own needs and those of the whole community, and for two horn players, who are to make the announcements that are made with horns at the command of the council of Agen, and in no other manner, except [f. 88r] the

88r] las cridas menudas de causas perdudas, e de tavernas, e d'autras cridas que·s podo e·s devo far, salvas las senhorias e las drechuras dels senhors e de la universitat d'Agen. E si ost se fazia de la ciutat, e de la universitat, e dels borcs d'Agen en fora, que .iiii. prohomes del cosselh d'Agen ano en la ost o en las osts, a caval cadaus, e que aio lors saumers en que porton armas a lors cors garnir, e als cavals, e·ls arcbalestas, e·ls cairels comunals, e·l trap, e la senhera, e·l senherer ab los trompadors de la vila d'Agen, e li meiss trompador i devo anar, liqual .iiii. prohomes de cosselh devo [f. 88v] traire las messios a lor obs meiss, e a lors messatges que obs lor auran, e als trompadors, e al senharer, de menjar, e de beure, e de lors cavalgaduras del borc e de la ciutat de la dicha universitat.

[CHAPTER LIII]

Aquest capitols parla cum lo cosselh d'Agen deu eslegir dels prohomes de la dicha universitat, de lor meiss, de cosselh, o dels notaris, o d'autres homes, de quals que·s volho de la dicha universitat, la on necessitatz sera per enviar foras de la dicha ciutat per los comunals negocis de la meissa universitat.[60]

E que aquel o aquilh que eslegitz seran per anar sian tengut e obligat per lo sagrament que [f. 89r] fachs auran al cosselh ses tota exceptio, si sas es de son cors, o si autra persona no era estada requesta per far aquela meissa anada de la dicha universitat, e que aquel o aquilh lo qual o li quals farion aquela anada juron sobre·ls sans evangelis de Dieu que ilh el negoci o els negocis el qual o els quals seran enviat, fassan e procuren per lor meiss e ab aquelas personas que poiran tot lo protenh, e tota la utilitat, e tot l'acreissement que far poiran a la dicha universitat, per aquo per que seran enviat, e per totas autras causas, e que laissen e esquivon tot dampnatge, e tota inutilitat, e tot amermament, de tots e de cadau de la dicha universitat e de [f. 89v] las franquessas de la dicha universitat, a lor leial poder a bona fe, e que menan aquel negoci o aquels negocis, no compron ni arrendon a temps peatge, ni renda, ni justizia, ni nulha juridictio de senhor ni de senhors de terra, e qui aital compra o arrendament faria que remases perjurs e infams per tostemps. E lo cosselh d'Agen fassa e pague las messios que aquel o aquilhs li qual serion enviat de las personas desus dichas per los comunals negocis de la dicha universitat farian, de men–jar, e de beure, e de loguers de bestias, e de tota messio que fessan per razo dels negocis per los quals serian enviat; e que si estavo .xx. dias continuatz o d'aqui [f. 90r] en sus, anan o tornan, o estan, que aquel o aquilh que seran enviat posco far cadaus de totz aquels que i iran, si pero logat no era per certa soudada, una rauba covenabla segont la persona. E que totas e cadauna las messios contengudas en aquest capitol, e de cada fachs contengut en aquest capitol e els autres capitols, que sobremontario .c. sols d'arnaldencs que lo cosselhs las traga per sotz e per lioras {*sic*} de la universitat, de la ciutat, e dels borcs

little public announcements [*cridas menudas*] for lost property and taverns and other announcements that can and should be made, saving the lordships and the rights of the lords and of the whole community of Agen. And if there were a military expedition [*ost*] of the city and the whole community and the suburbs of Agen outside the area [*en fora*], four men of the council of Agen go on the expedition or expeditions, each one on horseback, and with their pack animals to carry armor to protect them and their horses, and the communal crossbows and quarrels, and the tent and the town flag [*senhera*] and the flagbearer with the horn blowers of the town of Agen . And the said horn blowers are to go. These 4 goodmen of the council must [Folio 88 verso] be reimbursed [*traire*] expenses for their own needs and those of the messengers they need, and the horn blowers and the flagbearer for their food and drink and transportation [*cavalgaduras*] by the suburb and the city and the said community.

[CHAPTER LIII]

This chapter tells how the council of Agen should choose from among the goodmen of the said community, or from their own selves of the council, or from the notaries or other men, whomever they wish, of the said community when there is a need to send people out of the said city for the public business of the said com–munity.[61]

And how the person or persons chosen to go are obliged and required by their oath that [f. 89r] they have made to the council without any exception provided they are in good health, or if no other person had been requested by the said community to make this journey, and how the person or persons who are to make this journey swear on God's Holy Gospels that in the business fr which they are sent they will accomplish and procure, both they and all the persons they can {command}, all the advancement [*protenh*] and the useful things [*utilitat*] and all the increase they can of the said community in the business for which they are sent and in all other matters, and that they avoid and prevent loss and harmful things [*inutilitat*] and all diminution [*amermament*] of each and every person of the said community and the [f. 89v] free–doms [*franquessas*] of the said community, to {the extent of} their honest power in good faith. And they must conduct the business or businesses without buying or giv–ing a deposit for a time payment [*no compron ni arrendon a temps peatge*] or revenue or justice nor any jurisdiction of a landowner or landowners, and whoever made such a purchase or deferrment, let him remain a perjurer and defamed for ever. And the council of Agen should cover [*fassa*] and pay the expenses that the person or persons who are sent from among the persons above mentioned incur for eating and drinking and for renting animals, and all the expenses they incurred by reason of the business on which they were sent. And if they were away for 20 days or more continuously, [f. 90r] while going or coming or staying since the person or persons were sent out, each one of all those who went could have an appropriate robe made, according to the person, unless they had been hired for a fixed sum. And concerning each and every expense contained in this chapter and in the other chapters that exceeded 100 arnaldenc sous, the council must make a levy for the sous and livres {expended} [*traga per sotz e per lioras*] from the community and the city and the suburbs of Agen,

d'Agen, e las pague a las personas e als locs als quals seran obligat de pagar tuchs ensems de cosselh, o l'aus de cosselhs per cossentiment dels autres companhos, aquel meiss an que seran de cosselh, e que de totas e sengles las dichas messios sion [f. 90v] creut per aquel sagrament que fachs auran a la dicha universitat lo dia que ilh auran receubut l'offici del cosselh, e que nulha deffensios no ·ls i posca estre messa. Empero si per alcu cas s'endevenia que no poguessan aver trachas las dichas messios dins lo meiss an que serian de cosselh, que lo cosselhs que apres seria eslegitz e fachs aqui meiss a la requesta d'aquel cosselh, o de l'aun, que un de lor sia tengutz de traire de la dicha universitat aquelas messios, e de pagar aqui on serian degudas.

[CHAPTER LIV]

Aquest capitols parla d'aquels qui vendo cubelotz de ven- [f. 91r] -denhas ni de recs, e es a ssaber que li cubelot de mujazo de vendenhas son e devo estre de .vi. saumadas grossas, e li rec de .v. saumadas e un barril, e aquel que vendra los cubelotz o de rec o de vendenhas que ·ls renda estancs, e barradz, e be entalucadz, e ses malvada doga e ses malvada pessa de fons, e aquel qui contradizera que aissi no o complisca al comprador o als compradors que fos tengutz a las senhorias de pagar .xii. diners de gatges per cada cubelot, e no fos tengutz lo vendeire si era mager o mendre lo cubelot un carter. [f. 91v]

[CHAPTER LV]

Aquest capitols parla del fagh del vi e de la vendenha.

Costuma es a Agen que tots borzes o borzeza d'Agen levans e colgans pusca metre vendenha en la vila d'Agen, en vendenhas de sas proprias vinhas, ab que las obre ab homes levans e colgans de la vila d'Agen, e que li home ab loscals las obraran torno la nugh jazer a Agen, e tots hom qui aia vinha dins los dex d'Agen pusca metre sa vendenha en la vila d'Agen en vendenhas. ¶ Item: que si nulhs borzes d'Agen avia mesters de vi vermelh a sos vis a colorar, e que non trobes a vendre dins la vila d'Agen, qu'en [f. 92r] pusca comprar dins los dex e que ·l meta en la vila dins Martror, e no d'aqui avant, e aquo que fassa ab voluntat dels senhors e del cosselh, e que jure sobre sens en las lor mas que dins la vila non troba a vendre. ¶Item: que totz borzes o borzeza d'Agen que aia vinada d'arenda ne pusca metre aquela vinada en la vila d'Agen dins Martror, ab que jure sobre sens al cosselh d'Agen que no ·l venda a mercaders ni a taverna, ni ·l mescle ab vis que vendes, mas que propriament lo beva dins son ostal ab sa mainada. E si negus hom d'on que ·s fos fazia contra las sobredichas cauzas, que pague .lxv. sols d'arnaldencs de gatge, so es a saber [f. 92v] lo

and pay them to the persons and the places where they are to pay, all together as a council, or one of the council at the consent of the other members [*companhos*], that same year when they are on the council, and each and every one of the said expenses should be [f. 90v] believed {i.e. unchal–lenged} because of the oath they swore to the said community on the day they received the appointment from the council, and no defense may be raised. However, if a case arose where they could not raise the money for the said expenses in the year when they were members of the council, then the council that was elected and installed afterwards, at the request of that council or of one of them, should be required to raise these expenses from the said community and pay them where they were owed.

[CHAPTER LIV]

This chapter speaks of those who sell vats [*cubelotz*] for wine [f. 91r] harvest [*vendenhas*], or storage [*recs*],[62] and it should be known that the vats for the fermentation for wine making are and should be 6 large *saumadas* in size, and the storage vats [*li rec*] 5 *saumadas* and one *barril*, and a person selling vats for grapes or for wine making must make them watertight and caulked [*baradz*] and well beveled [*entalucatz?*], and without a bad stave or a bad bottom piece, and a person admitting [*contradizera?*] that he did not do this for the buyer or buyers, would be required by the authorities [*senhorias*] to pay 12 deniers as a fine for each vat, and the seller would not be required to pay if it was a quart [*carter*] bigger or smaller than the {standard} vat. [f. 91v]

[CHAPTER LV]

This chapter speaks of the making [*fagh*] of wine and the wine harvest.

It is the custom in Agen that any man or woman resident bourgeois of Agen can bring his wine harvest [*vendenha*] into the town [*vila*] of Agen, harvested from his own vines, provided he works them with men resident in the town of Agen, and that the men with whom he works them come back at night to sleep in Agen. And any man who has a vineyard within the limits of Agen can bring his harvest into the town of Agen during the harvest period [*en vendenhas*]. ¶Item, if any bourgeois of Agen needed red wine to color his wine, and found none for sale in the town of Agen that [f. 92r] he could buy within the city limits,{then he} could bring{some} into the town of Agen before Martyrs day, and no later. And to do this he must have the consent of the lords and the council, and swear on the saints in their hands that he found none for sale in the town.¶Item any man or woman bourgeois of Agen who has wine paid as rent [*arenda*] cannot bring this wine into Agen before the Martyrs day, unless he or she swears on the saints to the council of Agen that he or she will not sell it to a merchant or a tavern nor mix it with wine he or she sells, but that he or she will drink it privately within his or her house and with his or her household. And if any man wherever he was from acted contrary to the above said things, he should pay 65 arnaldenc sous as a fine, that is to say [f. 92v] a third to the lord, a third to the town and a third to whoever saw it and reported it. And the wine that was left would be

ters al senhor, e ·l ters a la vila, e ·l ters a aquel qui o veira e o diria, e ·l vis que fos encors e versatz, e ·l vaichels en que ·l meihs vis seria ars el paiment d'Agen.

[CHAPTER LVI]

Aquest capitols parla si li senhor volio prendre borzes o borzeza d'Agen.

Negus borzes ni borzeza d'Agen no deu estre pres, ni restadz, ni mes en turment pels senhors, si no era per jutgament del cosselh d'Agen.

[CHAPTER LVII]

Aquest capitols parla del fach dels captals, e de las cumpanhias, e de las comandas que hom fa.

Si negus borzes o borzeza d'Agen bailava o liorava captal en cumpanhia a neguna [f. 93r] persona, que aquela persona que auria resseobud lo digh captal sia tenguda da rendre cumte al borzes o a la borzeza que ·l digh captal l'auria bailat dins .viii. dias que el, o sos heretz, o sos ordenhs, l'en requerion, precizament e ses tota defucha, e ses demandar libel, ni dia de cosselh, ni de resposta, ni de razonador, ni de-guna autre dilasio per que degun alonguer y pogues metre, mas que dins los .viii. apres la dicha requesta sia tengudz da redre cunte cum digh es desus, e de redre lo captal e ·l gahan que fagh n'auria, e que ·l borzes o la borzeza que ·l digh captal auria bailat no ·l sia tengudz de donar libel. ¶ Que si negus borzes o borzeza d'Agen bailava o liorava a neguna perssona alcuna comanda de diners o d'als, [f. 93v] que aquela perssona qui auria resseobuda la dicha comanda sia tenguda da rendre a la requesta d'aquel qui balada la i auria, o de son heret, o de son ordenh, dins .iii. dias que ilh l'en requerio, presizament, e ses tota defucha, e ses demandar libel, ni dia de cosselh, ni de resposta, ni de razonador. ¶ Que tostz {*sic*} hom e tota femna pusca venir a Agen en la feira e en las vendenhas saubs e segurs, e far son pro, si home o femna mort no i avia, o pres no ·l tenia, o foc no i avia mes, o forbanditz non era, si ades en contenent sigitz no era per forfagh que agues fagh en alcus locs.

[End of the *Costuma d'Agen*]

[CHAPTER LVIII (42)].

[This chapter is listed in the medieval Table of Contents, but there is no text for it. In the left margin, at this point, appears the notation in a much later hand: "42 Deficit."]

poured out and the container in which the said wine was would be burned on the Agen paving stones.

[CHAPTER LVI]

This chapter tells {what happens} if the lords want to arrest a man or woman bourgeois of Agen.

No man or woman bourgeois of Agen may be arrested or taken into custody nor put to the torture by the lords unless it was by the judgment of the council of Agen.

[CHAPTER LVII]

This chapter speaks of partnership property [*captals*] and partnerships [*cumpanhias*] and limited partnerships [*comandas*] that are made.

If any man or woman bourgeois of Agen handed over or delivered property in partnership to any [f. 93r] person then the person who had accepted the said property would be required to render accounts to the man or woman bourgeois who had delivered to him the said property within 8 days of when he or his heirs asked for it, in full [*precizament*] and without any fraud, and without asking for a written complaint [*libel*] nor a counsel day a day for answering nor to find an advocate, nor any other dilatory {exception} by which he might prolong the matter. But within the 8 days after the said request he must be made to give an accounting as is said above, and to give back the property and the profit he made from it, and without the man or woman bourgeois who gave him the property having to give him a written complaint. ¶ That if any man or woman bourgeois of Agen gave or delivered to any person some limited partnership [*comanda*] in money or something other, [f. 93v] that person who had received the said limited partnership shall be required to give it back at the request of the person who had delivered it to him (or of his heirs or assigns) within 3 days that he requested it, in full and without fraud, and without asking for a written complaint nor a day for taking counsel or answering or finding an advocate. ¶ That any man or woman may come to Agen on feast days and during the wine harvest safe and sure and pursue his business [*far son pro*] unless he had killed a man or woman or was holding them prisoner or had set a fire, and had not been banished or was being hotly pursued for some offense he had committed somewhere.

---

[1] These words are in red ink, and appear to have been added in a space above the word "Conoguda" by a contemporary hand, but are not part of the original conception. Similar chapter headings, in Latin, appear above the beginnings of chapters I-III and V, but no others.

[2] The wording of the Prologue resembles that found in a charter of 1221, given by the future Raymond VII of Toulouse (count from 1222 to 1249), see Appendix A.

[3] The Agen citizens insisted on several occasions that the new count's oath had to precede that of the citizens. See charter CXXIV in Appendix A. The same clause is found in other customary compilations in the south-west, e.g. in the *Coutume de Marmande* (Ourliac and Gilles, vol 1, pp. 102-104) and see Bisson, p. 271.

[4] These two sentences are in Latin in the text, and the first is inscribed in a separate compartment next to the full-page initial letter I.

[5] Rigaudière notes that the title of *universitat* is sought by towns. The word *universitat(z)* seems to refer to the whole population, including that of the city itself, and those in the *borcs* outside the wall. Another name for this is Latin *commune*, for which the cognate "community" seems preferable to the ambiguous "university." "Community" or "whole community" is therefore used throughout to translate "*universitat(s)*".

[6] A note at the bottom of the page, in a much later hand, glosses the word *regnet* as "arrière garde, garde de nuit." This word does not appear in the Raynouard or Lévy dictionaries. In manuscripts B, N and S it appears as "regart." which the Petit Lévy gives as "danger." This is the meaning that is adopted here.

[7] The local currency is the arnaldenc sou. See Nony, Daniel in the Bibliography.

[8] *Mestura* (Mod. Fr. méteil) is wheat mixed with rye. *Passe-méteil* is defined as two-thirds wheat to one-third rye.

[9] A variant translation might be "salt master."

[10] On the river Baïse, near Lavardac.

[11] On the river Lot, where it joins the Garonne.

[12] Perhaps "between the Lot and the Garonne" means to refer to the position of Aiguillon, which lies between the two rivers; or perhaps it means that to go to the upper reaches of the Lot from Agen a boat first has to go downstream on the Garonne to the confluence of the two rivers.

[13] The verb *enquerre* seems to have a special meaning in Agen. It clearly does not mean "sue," since the recourse to the court comes only after the "enqueste" has failed. Moullié construes the word in the sense of "at–tempted settlement," for which he uses the French expression: "interpellation amiable."

[14] MS 42 makes no chapter break here. But Moullié's edition does, so to keep the chapter numbers aligned here, I have started a new chapter.

[15] These three letters appear at the beginning of a line, and repeat the last three letters of the last word on the line before. They appear to be a slip of the pen. None of the other manuscripts or editions contains these letters.

[16] The word q[ue] appearing in this sentence appears not to be a relative pronoun. I take it to be the "que" that sometimes precedes a verb in the main clause in Gascon.

[17] *Terra garda* is the showing of some property to a party so that he knows what is in dispute. *Reire garda* (or reiregarda) appears to be a showing by the adverse party. Old French is *jour de veue.*

[18] Since this manuscript is the "swearing copy" of the Agen customary, this mention of the "Holy Gospels" is actually a self reference. The swearing page was at f.s 7v and 8r of MS 42.

[19] The paragraph mark ¶ is often used in this manuscript as a marker of some comment or corollary, or at some other division of the text (see especially chapter 50).

[20] In Roman law, a person receiving an unfavorable judgment later shown to be false can claim "*injuria,*" 'outrage,' because his personal dignity was affected by the (false) judgment. A battery of a person was treated the same way, as an injuria. The word has persisted as the French "injure," with the narrower meaning of "verbal insult."

[21] The manuscript clearly says *caloniar*, not *calomniar*, but the meaning might be "false accusations" or "calum–ny" rather then "challenge."

[22] I have opted here to use the standard English term "vouch a warrantor." The warrantor is the person who can explain how a person came to be in possession of something: because the warrantor was the immediate past owner of the object, who sold it or gave it to the person whose ownership is now in question, and who calls upon him to explain how he acquired the object.

[23] *Liure* could have been translated "pound" since it consists of sixteen ounces. The £ sign used to mean "pounds sterling" derives from the L of *livre* in British coinage.

[24] *Leial* has the meaning of "exact, right, precise, fair, legal, reliable, honest."
[25] The word *drechura* is translated elsewhere as "right(s)" but here that seemed insufficient. It is hard to define justice, especially using a single word. The classical definition of *Iustitia* in the first sentence of the *Institutes*, part of Justinian's definitive formulation of Roman law, which might have been known to the writer of this chapter of the *Costuma d'Agen*, suggests that justice is "an unswerving and perpetual determination to acknowledge all men's rights." See Birks and McCleod. The root of the word *drechura* is *drech*, or right, so that it seemed appropriate to retain that in the translation.
[26] For a discussion of accidents in sports, etc., see Beaumanoir §1957.
[27] The word "bourgeois" has been used to translate the Occitan *borzes*. The meaning of *borzes*, however, appears to be "resident of one of the *borcs* of Agen." This is clear from chapter XX (f. 51v), where the words *ciutat* and *borcs* (resumed under the words *uila d'Agen*) are followed in the same sentence by the words *ciutada* and *borzes* (resumed as *home en la vila d'Agen).* There is no English word ready to hand to translate this word *borc* so I have used the word "suburb." The reader should thus be aware that a "bourgeois" is a resident of a "suburb" rather than of the "city" of Agen. An inhabitants of Agen itself are referred to in Occitan as *ciutada* which I have translated as "citizen." The word "resident" used in this sentence of the translation represents the Occitan word *habitant.*
[28] *Ordener* may be just another word for an executor.
[29] This very convoluted sentence, full of subjunctives and strings of "or" conjunctions, is hard to translate. Whichever way this translator tried to construe it, it seemed that there was something missing that had to be supplied. Yet the other editions shed no light on how to decipher the sentence. The message seems to be, however, that the rule aims to keep real property out of the hands of the clerical class, or indeed out of the hands of any but the middle class.
[30] See footnote to *injuria* at n. 19.
[31] Prescription (a prescriptive right) is the protection a holder of property is given after a certain time of hold–ing (a number of years). After this time a person claimimg to be the real owner cannot sue the current holder for possession.
[32] Much of the substance of this chapter is already contained in a Charter of 1221, see Introduction p. XI and Appendix A.
[33] It is hard to see how the last part of the sentence (after "if the wife died") connects with what goes before. There seems to be a parallel, "if the husband died first," followed by "If the wife died first," in which case perhaps there is a lacuna at the point of this note.
[34] It is hard to see how the last part of the sentence (after "if the wife died") connects with what goes before. There seems to be a parallel, "if the husband died first," followed by "If the wife died first," in which case perhaps there is a lacuna at the point of this note.
[35] Probably Lafox, about five miles south-east of Agen.
[36] Probably Beauville, about fourteen miles east-north-east of Agen.
[37] Marmande, on the Garonne, about thirty-one miles north-west of Agen by road, longer by river.
[38] The word *estatgers* means something like " The person staying for a while," or "the temporary resident." Another possibility would be "renter."
[39] The different manuscripts are in disagreement here (A: *desfaghs*, B: *defrach*, N: *desfagh* and S: *desflaghs* or *desfaghs.* I adopt the reading of N, in the sense of "undoing," or "successful contestation."
[40] The manuscript here reads *a lau*, which might be interpreted as *a l'aü*, since the pronoun is masculine.
[41] The marginal note in the manuscript, "Un homme peut tester à 14 and et une femme à 12," suggests that an earlier reader believes that the *no d'aqui en aval* and the *no d'aqui en jos* both have the same meaning. They suggest that the writer sees time as a point, with a before and after, rather than as a river flowing onwards, where down is later. Twelve and fourteen were the respective minimum ages at which women and men could legally do certain things under Roman law.
[42] The word dels which looks like a Modern French partitive article, seems out of place here. However, it appears this way in Moullié, and in mss. B, N, and S.
[43] The modern perch (also calleda rod or pole) is sixteen and a half feet, or five and a half yards.
[44] For *depart* Moullié and B have *de part*, and S has *part.*
[45] For *taula* Moullié suggests "usage personnel." In a similar oath a few lines later the Old Occitan text says: "per sos ops propriament," which is much closer to "for his personal use," and I have seen these two expressions as different.
[46] The different manuscripts are in agreement about this wording, but the meaning is unclear. The word *empres* does not appear anywhere else in this text.
[47] That is, make the complaint.

[48] That is, insists on having the complaint heard.
[49] That is, proportionately to his wealth.
[50] These last few words translate a few words that appear much lower in the transcribed text (near the end of f. 77v).
[51] These three occurrencs of the word *tornas* are the only ones in this manuscript. I conjecture the translation "in addition" although it seems possible that *tornas* could be something to do with reversion.
[52] Tropamer reads *mano*, but Moullié reads *movo* and Barckhausen reads *mavo*.
[53] The following word in the ms, *instruments*, is the only occurrence of the word. Except in this sentence, I have routinely translated the word *carta* by the English "instrument," because in English the cognate "charter" has a different meaning, and also because the Latin word that is used in the *Coutumes de Toulouse* is *instrument*, e.g. "cum publico instrumento per publicum Tholose notarium confecto," Henri Gilles, *Les Coutumes de Toulouse (1286) et leur premier Commentaire (1296)* (Toulouse: Recueil de l'Académie de Législation, 1969. p. 89), which is clearly the kind of written document referred to here in the *Costuma d'Agen*. Note, however, that the *Coutumes de Toulouse* also use the word carta, e.g. "cum carta vel sine carta", (ib. p. 91).
[54] Moullié and manuscripts B, and S all read *comunals* here.
[55] The break here is like that for the beginning of a new chapter, with a large initial *D*, but the editions of Tropamer and Moullié do not commence a new chapter here.
[56] The text translated in parentheses appears as an addition in the lower right margin of the manuscript.
[57] This curious manner of estimating the damages is copied from Roman law as seen in the Institutes 4.4.7 "Praetores permittebant ipsis qui iniuriam passi sunt eam aestimare" and also in the twelfth-century Exceptiones Petri: "Iuret prius ille qui iniuriam passus est, pro quanto nollet iniuriam istam sibi esse illata." The idea is found also in the mid-twelfth century Old Occitan *Lo Codi*, at 9.23.§1: aitant cant uol iurar aquel hom a cui fon li auta faita, per cant el no volria adonc, cora li auta li fo faita aver receubuda aquella auta ..." See Derrer, Felix, in the Bibliography. The use of the word *iniuria* in connection with the word *aunta* recalls the same co-occurrence in Old Occitan in *Lo Codi* Book 9.
[58] The error in the word *drchs* (for *drechs*) lends credence to the conclusion that something has gone awry with this last sentence. Perhaps the word *facha* that looks like a feminine past participle is actually a present subjunctive used as an imperative. Or perhaps the word *es* has been omitted between *aisso* and *facha*. Cf at the top of page 39r for a similar sentence. On the other hand, Moullié and Tropamer give a text that is essentially the same as Ms. 42, and the former does not note any variants.
[59] The words in parentheses are a marginal addition the text. There is here a large colored capital, but the editions of Tropamer and Mouillié do not start a new chapter.
[60] The *Livre juratoire* makes no break here. Moullié and Tropamer treat this first sentence as a preamble.
[61] Tropamer and Moullié both consider that the heading ends here, but the sentence does not appear to stop. In the *Livre juratoire*, there is a sign like a tilde, at the level of the line, as if to mark a greater break that those indicated by the period or colon. This mark does not appear anywhere else in the manuscript.
[62] Tropamer and Moullié both treat the text up to this point as a heading.

[Bottom of f. 93r] Quas quidem consuetudines sive costumas ac omnia supra scripta et in dicto libro contenta grata rata habentes et grata ea laudamus[1] ratificamus approbam[us][2] [f. 94r][3] ac ex[4] nostra certa scientia auctoritate regis qua fungimur in hac parte et gr[ati]a sp[eci]a[li][5] tenor[e] presentamus confirmamus mandantes Seneschallo Agennensi civibus que justiciariis regiis praesentibus et futuris aut eorum locum tenentibus et cuilibet eorum(?)[6] quathenus consules uniuersitatis et habitatores[7] civitatis Agenni supra dicta quorum X[8] consuetudinibus seu costumis supra scriptis ac X[9] praesentibus gvaX[10] confirma[m?]ont[11] uti patissiue(?)[12] faciant et gaudent ipsos in contrarium nullatenus molestant aut a quo quam molestari quomodo libri promittentes[13] quod ut perpetuae firmitatis robur obtineat praesentas litteras Sigilli nostri jussimus impressione muniri in aliis dicti dum modi[14] jure et alieno in omnibus semper salvo. Datum Agenni

[f. 94v] Anno Domini millesimo ccc° sexagesimo nono[15] (1369) mensis februarii.

Nos autem consuetudines sive costumas supra scriptas et omnia et singula alia insupra scriptis Lvue(?) (   )[16] contenta rata et grata habentes eas laudamus, ratificamus approbamus et confirmamus ac de novo consulibus universitatis et habitatoribus Civitatis nostrae agenni Supra scriptae pro se et Successoribus Suis in perpetuum pro nobis et successoribus nostris consedimus (sic) et donamus auctoritate nostra regia et certa Scientia et grata spali(?) p[er] pntes[17] mandam[us] seneschallo judicibus majori pro

---

[1] The *l* of *laudamus* looks more like a *v*, but the phrase appears later on f. 94v where the letter is clearly an *l*.

[2] At the end of the text on this page appears the blue oval stamp inscribed with the words "Bibliothèque d'Agen."

[3] ff 94 and 95 are of paper, not parchment, amd are the only paper folios in the manuscript containing text. One other paper folio appears as an end paper inside the back cover.

[4] The copyist seems to have been unable to understand this word, and to have merely drawn into his copy a picture of what he saw before him. I will call this a "drawn word." It is possible to read the drawing as "ex," as Moullié has the word.

[5] These two drawn words have been adopted from Moullié.

[6] Moullié reads this drawn word and the preceding as "consiliariis eorum." The scribe must have misread "consiliariis" as "cuilibet," and then he did not understand the next word. It is possible to discern under the drawing the outline of "eorum."

[7] The endings of "universitatis" and "habitatores" have been overwritten with a correction.

[8] Another drawn word. Moullié has "intererit et tangere poterit." In the drawn word it is possible to see "intererit" but the other words given by Moullié are simply missing. X signifies the presence of some illegible writing.

[9] Another drawn word. Moullié has "nostris."

[10] Another drawn word. Moullié has "gratiâ."

[11] The text seems to read "confirmaont" with a large tilde over the a. Moullié reads "confirmatione."

[12] A drawn word. Moullié has "pacificè."

[13] For "quomodo libri promittentes," Moullié has "quomodolibet molestari permittent."

[14] For "dicti dum modi" Moullié has "domini mei."

[15] In Moullié, the year is given as "MCCCLXIX°"

[16] Drawn word, followed by an empty parenthesis. In the formula that opens the first confirmation, the words at this point are: "in dicto libro."

[17] Drawn words with an abbreviation mark. They could be: "speciali per praesentes"

ordinario Agennensibus. Seneschalles judicibus justiciariis Ministris et officiariis nostris et aliis in regno nostro constitutis praesentibus [f. 95r] et futuris velevze[18] loca tenentibus et eorum cuilibet quathenus prefactos consules; universitatem et habitatores modernos et futuros dictis consuetudinibus pro ut superius Exprimiuntur(?) et dantur(?)[19] qualibus ad plenum gaudeat et uti faciant et permittant. et si forsan[20] contigerit aliquid in Contrarium fieri seu attemplari, id ad statum pristinum perducant inditate (i). Quod ut perpetuo firmitatis robur obtineat, praesentes litteras Sigilli nostri iussimus impressione muniri. Jure nostro in aliis et in omnibus quolibet alieno, Semper Salvo. Actum apud Vincennas, anno Dom[i]ni millesimo trecentesimo septuagesimo regni nostri Septimo mense maii.

(i) mot de la basse latinité qui signifie Sans délai.[21]

[18] A drawn word where the three e's and the l and the z are fairly plain. Could the words have been "de Iure?"
[19] These two words are drawn and the second includes an abbreviation mark.
[20] The last minim of "forsam" seems to have been crossed out.
[21] These words in French are added in a smaller and possibly different hand and between two red lines at the bottom of the text. The word to which they refer is indicated by the mark (i) in the text, which is added by the copier of the Latin text and not, apparently, added later.

[ff 94 and 95 are paper. They contain the end of the confirmation of Louis d'Anjou and the confirmation of Charles V, see pp. 93-94. The paper has been given a ruled frame in pencil, later redone in red. The scribe is copying a text, and does not always read well or understand what he reads. Where he is really puzzled, he simply draws a picture of what he is copying. If the MS A can be found, it will be possible to see if that was the source text.]

[f. 96r]
Rolle (?) de Messieurs les Juratz de la ville d'Agen qui se sont ... le vingtseptiesme de decembre gbic trente trois (1623?) [list of 19 names]

[f. 96v]

[list of 23 names]

[f. 97r]

[8 groups of three names, marked with year, from 1629 to 1636.]

[f. 97v]

[6 groups of three names, marked with year, from 1636 to 1642.]

[f. 98r]

[7 groups of three names, marked with year, from 1643 to 1649.]

[f. 98v]

[6 groups of three names, marked with year, from 1650 to 1655.]

[f. 99r]

[A group of three names and some other writing for 1655, then groups of three names marked 1656-1658, then four names (one crossed out) for 1659.]

[f. 99v]

[4 groups of three names for the years 1660-1663, with three lines crossed out between 1661 and 1662.]

[f. 100r]

[4 groups of three names, from 1664 to 1667.]

[f. 100v]

[4 groups of three names, from 1668 to 1671.]

[f. 101r]

[4 groups of three names, from 1664 to 1667.]

[f. 101v]

[4 groups of three names, from 1675 to 1678.]

[f. 102r]

[2 groups of three names, from 1679 to 1680, followed by smeared erasures for about one quarter of the page.]

[f. 102v]

[On Sept 15, 1681 a group of 6 names, sept 8 1682 three names, on Sept 15 1683, three names, 1684 three names, 1685 three names.]

[f. 103r]

[4 groups of three names for the years 1686-1688, and a group of six for 1689.]

[f. 103v]

[4 groups for the years 1689 (sic) to 1691. Two of the names from the six mentioned for 1689 on f. 103r reappear for that year on f. 103v.]

[f. 104r]

[3 groups of 6 names for 1692 to 1694.]

[f. 104v]

[3 groups of 6 for the years 1695-97.]

[f. 105r]

[For 1698, 4 names,for 1699 4 names, for 1700 4 names.]

[f. 105v]

[For 1701 four names (one crossed out), for 1702 four names. for 1703 4 or 5 names, for 1704 4 names.]

[f. 106r]

[For 1704 no names, for 1705 4 names, for 1706 6 names, for 1707 6 names, for 1708 3 or 4 names.]

[f. 106v]

[No text, pumiced and patched. This is the last folio of the manuscript.]

APPENDICES

APPENDIX A

This appendix includes the text of four charters from Agen. These charters were published by Adolphe Magen, and Georges Tholin, see Bibliography. These editors supply the heading (here in bold). The following short paragraph of each text (in Modern French) is a summary provided by the editors of these charters. Then follows the text, in Latin or Old Occitan.

Charter XI (p. 14) August 1221

Charte de Raymond, fils de Raymond VI, comte de Toulouse.

Confirmation des coutumes et octroi de divers privilèges à la ville d'Agen.

Ramons, fils del senhor Ramon, per la gracia de Deu dug de Narbona, comte de Tolosa, marches de Proensa et filhs de la dona regina na Johana, a totz aquels que aquestas letras veiran e ausiran, saluz en nostre senhor. Nos demostran a la nostra universitad per las presens letras que nos, per nos e per nostres successors, al maior e al coselh e a la universitad d'Agen *autrejam els confirmam totas lors costumas aissi que melhs les an agudas e tengudas ilh ni li lor ancessor ab los nostres ancessors, e melhs, si melhs podian, a l'entendament del coselh e dels autres proshomes d'Agen; e si, sobre las costumas de la ciutad d'Agen se movia contrast entre nos els ciutadas o entre los ciutadas e nostre badles (sic), nos ne creirem los .XII. proshomes del coselh; e si coselh no avia en la vila, nos ne creirem los .XII. proshomes de la meissa vila, que sian de bona renomnada, sobre lor sagrament que aisso que il autrejaran que sia costuma que nos o crezem e o autrejam e o tenem per ferm per nos e per los nostres*; e sobre tot aisso, autrejam e cofermam als sobredits ciutadas per nos e per los nostres en durabletad e per costuma que ja nulh temps no trairem hostadges ni n demandarem de la vila d'Agen, ni tort ni forsa no lur farem, ni oltra la costuma nols iram nos ni hom per nos, ni nulh home en la vila d'Agen no pendrem, ni de fora, que sia borzes de la ciutad d'Agen, si no o fasiam per jutgament del cosselh; e autrejam en durabletad als sobredits ciutadas que nos ni hom per nos ni per les nostres en la vila d'Agen castel no farem; e autrejam en durabletad als sobredits ciutadas que de totas las mercadarias, sia o blads, o vis, o autras causas que passen per nostra terra vas on que s sia per le dreit peatge que hom solia pendre el temps de nostre aviol; e sobre tot aisso autrejam e volem que totz hom de la vila d'Agen passe a Marmanda ab .IIII. diners del peatge del tonel del vi, e ab .I. diner de la conqua del blad, dor (sic) ques sia le bladz nil vis, e tat autra mercadaria passe ab lo dreit peatge aissi quo era acostumad el tems del rey Andrig; e totz homo (sic) que compre blad ni vi d'Agen passe a Marmanda, aissi que sobredit es, ab .IIII. diners del tonel del vi e ab .I. diner de la conqua del blad; e totz aquetz sobredits coventz e autreiaments non avem plivid (sic) e mandad, e jurad sobre sants evangelis que aissi o tingam e o compliam, quo sobredit es, per nos e per les nostres, per ara e per totz tems; e per que aisso plus ferm sia, nos avem faita sagelar la present carta ab le nostre sagel, e la avem faita sagelar al capitol de Tolosa del lor Sagle de Tolosa, els avem donads a mandadors que aissi o tingam que sobredit es. Aisso fo tot pauzad e autrejad en la ciutad de Tolosa .VII. dias a l'issid del mes d'Aost en dimercles, en l'an de la encarnacio de nostre Senhor M^{o}CC^{o}XXI°. [My emphasis]

Charter XLVI (p. 67) July 1248

Confirmation de privilège, par Raymond VII, comte de Toulouse

Il s'agit du privilège octoyé aux Agenais de ne payer au seigneur tailles ni quêtes, si ce n'est de leur plein gré.

Noverint universi presentes litteras inspecturi, quod nos Ramundus,Dei gracia comes Tholose, marchio Provincie, permittimus et concedimus, per nos et per omnes successores nostros civibus et toti (sic) universitati Agenni presentibus et futuris, quod ipsos et omnes successores eorum in perpetuum, infra civitatemAgenni et extra in cunctis locis, tenebimus *in illis libertatibus et bonis consuetudinibus* in quibus ipsos et ante–cessores eorum antecessores nostri et nos tenuimus temporibus retroactis, profitentes et recognoscentes quod, in civibus Agenni supradictis, univerasliter vel singulariter, quistam, talliam, vel mutuum non habebimus, nisi ipsi talliam nobis vellent dare vel mutuum facere de eorum spontanea voluntate. In cujus rei testimonium et majorem firmitatem, nos R. comes supradictus, presentes litteras fecimus sigilli nostri munimine roborari. Datum apud Moysiacum, quinto nonas julii, anno Domini millesimo ducentesimo quadragesimo octavo. [my emphasis]

Charter CXII (p. 188) December 1298

Vidimus par les Consuls d'Agen:

1. De lettres de Philippe-le-Bel, confirmant les privilèges accordés aux habitants d'Agen par le comte Raymond.
2 De l'ordonnance de Guillaume, trésorier d'Anjou, enquêteur royal, reconnaissant le privilège acquis aux Agenais de n'être point jugés hors de leur sénéchaussée.

Noverint universi presentes litteras inspecturi quod nos, consules civitatis Agenni, vidimus, legimus et diligenter inspeximus et de verbo ad verbum transcribi fecimus quasdam litteras sigillo et contra sigillo illustrissimi principis domini Philippi, Dei gratia Francorum regis cum cera viridia in pindenti sigillatas, et alias litteras sigillo venerabilis et discreti viri, domini Guillhelmi, thesaurii Andeguavensis, diciti domini nostri regis clerici, inquisitis in Vasconia et Agennensio … tenor vero litterarum … sequitur in hunc modum: Philippus dei gracia, etc. [1] … Guillhelmus, thesaurarius Andegavensis … Noveritis quod vocato coram nobis dicto Bernardo, *visisque privilegiis*

[1] The editors claim that the document referenced here is no. XCVIII of their volume, but this cannot be right, since that document begins "Rotbertus, comes Attrebatensis in partibus Tholosanae, …". However documents, XCVI and XCVII both begin "Philippus, Dei gratia Francorum rex, …" The first of these confirms the customs of Agen, quoting the charter of Raymond VII of Toulouse in 1248 (published in the same collection as no. XLVI, see above). The second confirms the charter confirming the Customs given by Raymond VI in 1221 (contained in the same volume as Charter no. XI see above). The events leading up to this Charter began when some citizens of Agen complained that they were being summoned outside of Agen, in Cahors, and that their customs, approved by the king, did not permit this procedure. The inquisitors eems satisfied that the privilege exists and orders the seneschal of Quercy not to proceed against them.

et libro consuetudinum Agenni, et juramentis plurium proborum hominum receptis, ...ordinavimus ut vobis ... scriberemus quod civitates Agenni extra districtum civitatis Agenni ... contra privilegia et consuetudines eorumdem, non traheretis nec citari faceretis ... [my emphasis]

Charter CXXIV (p. 210) March 1301 (o.s.)

Extraits de trois articles de la Coutume, délivrés sous le sceau des consuls.

Le premier, correspondant au chapitre XVI du texte imprimé,[2] est relatif à l'amende applicable à ceux qui se sont rendus coupables de coups et blessures, et au supplice réservé au meurtrier, lequel doit être enterré vivant sous le cadavre de sa victime.
Le deuxième, -- chapitre XVII, -- constate le droit des consuls de connaître, concurremment avec le bailli du suzerain, des causes criminelles.
le troisième, -- prologue du texte imprimé, -- reconnaît au témoignage de douze prud'hommes de la ville le pouvoir d'autoriser les points douteux de la Coutume.

Noverint universi presentes litteras inspecturi, quod nos, consules civitatis Agenni, de verbo ad verbum transcribi fecimus *de libro consuetudinum civitatis Agenni* [my emphasis], tria capitula in dicto libro contenta et scripta, quorum unius sequitur tenor in hunc modum:
Si lo senher a clam d'alcu hom etc. (*Chapitre* XVI.)
Tenor vero alterius capituli sequitur in hunc modum:
Lo senher, o sos senescalx, o sos balles, etc (*Chapitre* XVII.)
Tenor vero tertii capituli sequitur in hunc modum:
Conoguda e manifesta causa sia, etc. (*Prologue.*)
In cujus rei testimonium nos, consules predicti, sigillum nostrum et universitatis Agenni presenti transcripto duximus apponendum, ad majoris roboris firmitatem. Datum Agenni, die martis post festum beati Gregorii, anno Domini M° CCC° primo. [13 march 1302 n.s.]

[2] The editors are referring to the 1850 printed edition of Moullié, the only one that had appeared up to that point.

APPENDIX B

Transcription of "new" chapters from MS S[1]

S 1 E si nulhs hom o femna esta ab senhor i era malaus o malauta en aquela estaria de tant de temps quant seria estatz malaus o malauta li enmendaria per .I. dia dos apres lo terme dar ta(n)t [for d'aitant] bo temps cum si seria estat malaus o malauta si ·l senher lo fazia la messio.[2]

S 2 Si alcus comprava vi a Agen lo vendeire lo deu tener entro a la sent Johan Babtista e d'aqui en la esta a l'aventura del cumprador. E quant vendra al dig terme lo vendeires lo deu aoilhar e d'aqui en la esta a l'aventura del cumprador. E si lo vis se corria dins lo digh terme per fauta de doga o de seucle o de front lo vendeires[3] n ·es tengut. E si alcu mal prendia lo vis que hom agues fagh per mal, lo vendeire no n'es tengut ab que iure sobre sans avangelis que non es faghs per son consentiment ni per autrui que el saubos si en autra guia proar no lo podia. E si aventura i avenia de foc o que la maio cazos e cruses lo tonel o per barregh de vila o de fagh comunal de vila, o que hom lo prezes per destenher foc, es per maitat la perda. E quant vindra al terme del vin tener e los aura aolhatz d'aqui en la si nazia mucs aigres o puiritz[4] lo vendeires no n'es tengutz.

S 3 Si dui fraire o pluzors son e l'aun d'aquel gaanha en mercadaria o en als e li autri fraire no aian re gaanhat o enqueras aguessan li autri fraire gastada partida de la heretat de lor paire o de lor maire es costuma d'Agen e dregh escriutz que tugh li fraire partiran tot aquel gaanh sol que li fraire no aian partit la heretat paternal e maternal exceptada troba o don o causas dadas en dot per molher si la prendia que d'aquo non es tengutz lo fraire dar part.

S 4 Si alcus hom loga una maio d'autre e hom li penhora en la maio per aquel de cui el l'aura logada si l'estatgers vol estar segon la costuma d'Agen lo bales lo deu redre sas penhoras e l'estager deu pagar cada mes [*i a per aquo si l'estatgers pagua al creedor cada mes*][5] per aitant quant sera lo loguer de la maio l'an al creedor per lo qual lo bailes l'aura penhorat e que tant caira del loguer de la maio quant pagara al creedor cada mes, aissi cum digh es; e no caira del deute que ·l senher de la maio deu al creedor, mas be caira del loguer de la maio a l'estatger; e es a ssaber que si l'estatger de la maio a pagat tot lo loguer de la maio[6] quant aquella penhora sera facha cada mes aissi cum desus es digh, a-

---

[1] These chapters correspond to chapters 55-59 of Tropamer's edition of the Noubel manuscript. Chapers S1-S3 correspond to sections 88-90 of the Montpezat customary. S, N, and the Montpezat manuscript are the only manuscripts that contain these chapters. Only S and N contain chapters S4-5. The permission of the Royal Library, Stockholm, to whom the original manuscript S belongs, is gratefully acknowledged.

[2] The version of this chapter in the Monpezat customs is somewhat plainer:
"Item si hom o femna qui esta ab senhor loguat es malaus dins lo terme qu'el deu servir e li senhor li fa la metio en la malauzia, que aquel o aquela lo rendra dos dias per .I. apres lo meis terme, en aytant lo temps cum seria estat malaus." Orliac and Gilles, vol. 2, p. 111.

[3] Here Ms N has "no" which seems like a wrong avoidance of blame, The Montpezat provision is like that in MS S where the seller takes the risk of spoilage up to a certain moment marked by the verb *aoilhar*.

[4] Here MS N reads: "si vazia muos o agres o puirits" (Tropamer p. 140) and the Montpezat customary in the Ourliac and Gilles transcription reads "si s'endevenia mut o agres o pobritz,"

[5] Missing words supplied from MS N.

[6] The words *a pagat tot lo loguer de la maio* are missing in MS N.

quel an cumplit l'estatger deu estar tant oltra ·l terme per cant cum el aura pagat oltra lo loguer de la maio e aisso fazen lo bailes penhorar no li deu ni ·l senher de la maio gitar no l'en pot entre sa estaria n'a complida.

S 5 Negus hom d'Agen no ·s deu combatre per si ni per autrui de negu fagh don hom l'apele si en autra manera per jutjament de cort s'en vol defendre si per sa voluntat a la batalha no se obligava ni ·l senher ni autre destrenher no l'en deu. E si i avenia que batalha fos arramida entre ciutadas o borgues d'Agen o entre ciutadas o borgues d'Agen[7] e autres de foras per agradabblas voluntatz d'una part e d'autre e que las partidas a far li batalha agradablament si obliguesso, deu estre aissi fach, so es assaber que l'apelat se deu antar ab quals armas se volra combatre e deven estre datz .XL. dias a las partidas per iudicios dins los quals aion cercadas e parelhadas lors armas e las armas devon estre prezentadas en cort d'una part e d'autre dins los digh .XL. dias; e deven estre pageladas aquelas armas que sion d'un lonc, so es a saber lansas e cotels e espazas e massas e baston. E si la batalha era sobre dezeret de terra o de possessio sobre autre fagh que no ssia murtres o traissios o laironessis o crims o d'altre fagh don lo cors e l'aver e las cauzas d'aquel qui seria apelatz de crim serian encors al senhor per los encorremens que ·l senher deu aver dels fors faghs don parla desobre el capitol que comensa enaissi: Si negus hom o femna metia foc etcetera.

Translation of "new" chapters from MS S.

S1. And if any man or woman is employed by a lord and was sick during that employment, then for as much time as he or she was sick he or she would make up the time {by working} two days for one after the end of the employment in as good weather as if he or she had been sick when the lord was taking in the harvest.[8]

S2 If someone bought wine in Agen the seller should keep it until the feast of St. John the Baptist, and from then on it is at the risk of the buyer. And when the said date comes, the seller should top it off [*aoilhar*], and from then on it is at the risk of the buyer. And if the wine leaked out before that date, because of a defect in a barrel stave or a hoop or a barrel head, the seller is liable. And if anything bad happened to the wine that someone had caused in bad faith, the seller is not liable provided he swears on the holy gospels that it was not done with his agreement nor by anyone to his knowledge, if he cannot prove it any other way. And if there was an accident through fire or the house fell down and crushed the barrel or if there was a pillage of the town or some similar disturbance in the town, or it was taken to put out a fire, the loss is shared. And when the time for holding the wine comes, and it has been topped off, from then on if a bitter or rotten mother[9] began {to form}, the seller is not liable.

S3 If there are two or more brothers and one of them earns {money} by commerce or some other trade and the other brothers have not earned anything, or even if the other brothers had wasted a part of what they inherited from their father or their mother, the custom of Agen and written law is that all the brothers share in that

---

[7] The words *o entre ciutadas o borgues d'Agen* are missing in MS N

[8] Or, when the lord was paying their expenses.

[9] "Mother" is used here in its sense of "mother of vinegar, " Fr. "mère de vinaigre' a kind of starter (as in sourdough bread) that turns wine into vinegar. This meaning was suggested by Patric Sauzet, and is supported by the Latin name for mother, in this sense: mycoderma aceti, derived fron Greek mykhs (fungus)

gain if they have not partitioned their father's and mother's estate, with the exception of treasure trove or property given as a dowry for a wife if the man married her, for of these things the brother is not required to give a share.[10]

S4 If a man rents a house from another, and the house is seized as pledge for a debt by the person he rented it from, if the renter wants to stay in the house then according to the custom of Agen the *balle* must give him back his pledge and the renter must pay {money} every month up to the amount of the annual rental of the house to the creditor to whom the debtor pledged it and the same amount as the renter pays the creditor will be deducted from the rent each month, as was stated above. And it will not be deducted from the debt that the owner of the house owes the creditor, but it will be deducted from the renter's rent for the house. And it must be known that if the renter of the house has paid the whole of the rent for the house when the pledge is made, as was said above, then once the year is over the renter must stay in the house as long a time after the end of the period as he has paid above the rent of the house and at this time the *balle* should not take a pledge and the owner of the house cannot eject him even though he has completed his {original} term.

S5 No man of Agen must fight for himself or another for any issue on which he is appealed against if he wants to defend himself by order of the court in some other manner, unless he willingly obligated himself to the battle; and neither the lord nor any other person may force him. And if it came about that a battle was set up between citizens or bourgeois of Agen, or between ctizens or bourgois of Agen and others from outside, by free agreement on both sides, and the parties who were to do battle obligated themselves willingly, it should be done that way, that is to say that the appellee should select [*se antar*] which arms he wants to fight with, and the parties must be given forty days by court order within which to find and prepare their arms, and the arms must be presented to the court within the forty days by both parties; and these arms must be measured {to see} that they are the same length, that is lances and knives and swords and maces and clubs. And if the battle was over ownership or possession of land, about actions other than murder or treason or theft or or crime, or other actions such as those where the life and wealth of the person accused of a crime would be forfeit to the lord, for the seizures that the lord should have for the capital offenses spoken about in the chapter above which begins this way : "If any man or woman set fire to, etc." {Here, middle of Chapter XV}

[10] Brothers who have inherited from a deceased parent, but who have not yet partitioned (divided up) the estate are considered to be in a kind of partnership, with shared gains and losses

APPENDIX C

Description of the Manuscript by Professor M. Alison Stones, University of Pittsburgh. An expanded version of this description is to appear in: *Manuscripts Illuminated in France, Gothic Manuscripts 1260-1320*, London: Harvey Miller and Turnhout: Brepols, forthcoming.

Agen, Archives Départementales de Lot-et-Garonne, MS 42
Costuma d'Agen, in Occitan, between 1271 and 1279? Agen

Contains iv+3+106+ii ff. Ff. 1-93 are medieval (numbering skips from f. 12 to f. 16), ff. 94-95 a paper bifolium. The medieval section is numbered in 18c Roman numerals. 223x 156(145-75 to outer vertical ruling), 1 col, 22 lines, 21 lines f. 92v, 24 lines f. 93. Original rulings in faint leadpoint, double horizontals at top and bottom. The text block is bounded by double verticals ruled in red ink which I think were added at a later rebinding or during the retouching by D.B. in 1825. Some chapters are rubricated and numbered. Script in light brown ink, with additions on ff. 5v and 6, and ff. 81 to 93v, by an almost contemporary hand writing at a smaller scale. Champie initials in gold or silver on pink and blue backgrounds, with white flourishing, mostly the letter L. The last four in the Table of Contents (ff. 5v-6) are by a second decorator, corresponding to the change in scale in the script. Foliate initials with coloured backgrounds in pink or blue accompany the small miniatures, with dragons intertwined and white dots on leaves. A second hand is found from f. 81 to 93v, using gold backgrounds, gold balls on corners, and animal motifs, corresponding to the change of scale in the script. The two campaigns do not represent two widely different periods.

Two full-page miniatures (ff. 7v and 8); small miniatures or historiated initials at the openings of each chapter, with pink or blue plain or diaper backgrounds, and frames in plain gold and silver (tin ?), some touched up by 'D.B.', who signed f. Iv and dated his work 1825. Initials by a main artist with additions at the end (ff. 81-93v) by a second hand, using gold backgrounds, gold balls and animals; the drawing appears to be by the same hand throughout, with figures outlined in brown or black ink.

Table of Contents (ff. I verso-6): Beneath a pink arch, a seated scribe, bareheaded, in hooded robe writes at desk, two men standing before him, one wearing a cale (faces touched up by 'D.B.' who signed his initials and dated them 1825) (f. Iv); Gnadenstuhl Trinity (without Dove ?), very badly rubbed, in a mandorla, with the Virgin and St John kneeling at feet of God the Father, two angels censing, kneeling on the edges of the throne of God the Father, who holds up a TO globe and blesses, supporting Christ on the Cross with his raised arms; Evangelist symbols in spandrels (f. 7v); Virgin and Child enthroned, flanked by two angels holding stylised flowers; the Virgin shown nursing, and crowned, severely damaged (f. 8); Gospel pericopes: St John writing, eagle symbol below, with splayed wings (face of St John and wings of eagle touched up by 'D.B'?); I, foliate initial with nude male spewing forth foliage at bottom, intertwined dragons at top (f. 10); St Luke (face retouched) seated writing between two trees, ox symbol below; dragon border (f. 11); St Matthew (face retouched) seated writing between two trees, wearing wings, so no separate symbol is included (f. 11v); St Luke (face retouched) seated writing between two trees, grey lion symbol below, touched up, note 'Moi' in right margin, early 19th c. hand (f. 12); Prologue (Incipit prologus): Trinity: Two per-

sons on separate thrones, Dove between; I leaf initial with intertwined dragons top and bottom; blue wavy lines and red dots between the ruling lines (later additions, early 19th c.) (f. 17); Chapter 1 (Primum capitulum): The Lord of Agen swears his oath to the citizens: he sits before a group of nine male citizens, standing, of whom the foremost, wearing a cale, holds a book open to text pages; Q, foliate initial with dragon terminal (f. 17v); Chapter 2 (Secundum capitulum). The subsequent illustrations represent the various legal points described in the text. A complete description can be found in Alison Stones, Illuminated Manuscripts Made in France, Gothic Manuscripts 1260-1320 (forthcoming), no. VIII-14.

This is the most fully illustrated, and the earliest (according to Mouillé, 1851, 1853) of six surviving copies of the Costumas de Agen, and the swearing copy. Lauzun (1910, 2, citing Mouillé) lists the other places of preservation—but no shelf numbers—as in the Vatican, Bordeaux, Paris, another Agen manuscript and a sixth copy, also at Agen. (For an account of the manuscripts apparently still surviving, see Introduction, pp. IX-X)

The opening full-page miniatures of the Trinity and the Virgin and Child are now almost obliterated thanks to their having served as the recipients of the hands of swearing councillors from the last third of the thirteenth century to the Revolution, a situation also encountered in the early thirteenth-century *Livre rouge de Montauban*, Archives Departementales de Tarn-et-Garonne, AA 1, the *Livre vert* of Cahors (Cahors, Archives Municipales 1, on deposit at the Bibliothèque Municipale), the *Livre juratoire* of the bastide town of Cologne (Gers) (in a Private Collection), and the Registres consulaires de Limoges (Limoges, Archives Municipales AA 1). The Cahors and Cologne swearing pages are approximately contemporary with the Agen *Costumas*. These manuscripts are remarkable witnesses to civic consciousness in the south-west of France, to which the Customary of Toulouse of 1296 (Paris, Bibliothèque nationale de France, latin 9187) is also a significant testimony. During the thirteenth century the political situation of the Agenais was one of shifting allegiances. The region came into Angevin control in 1152 and in 1196 was acquired as a fief by Count Raymond VI of Toulouse as dowry for his marriage to King Richard's sister Joan. When Raymond VII died without male heir in 1249, Henry III tried to recover the Agenais but it was still a part of the county when the Toulousan inheritance fell to the French crown in 1271. It was acquired by Edward I at the Treaty of Amiens in 1279, on whose behalf William de Valence (c. 1230-1296), father of the likely owner of the Murthly Hours (Edinburgh, National Library of Scotland, 21000), represented his uncle in taking possession of Agen, founding the bastide of Valence during his sojourn in the region. Agen reverted to the French again in 1294. The most likely date for the production of Agen 42 is between 1271 and 1279 since the arms of England are not included among the banners in the military service miniature on f. 18v, where the arms of Agen, (*azure an eagle or* and *gules a castle or,* as on the seal of 1243) and Toulouse (*gules a cross or encircled with besants or)*, are shown. The sole mention of an overlord, the 'prince' in the context of seizures coming to the prince on f. 42 (Chapter 18), suggests that an earlier text may have been copied with this reference unchanged. It may be that this copy was made to reaffirm the citizens' rights and customs in the face of a new French overlord in 1271; it is possible that the later phase was done after 1274 or after 1294 though there is nothing in the text that would justify such a time-lag and the figure style is consistent throughout, as noted below. The inclusion of women wearing the 'touret' stylet of headgear would suggest that the major campaign took place in the 1270s rather than the

1290s (no women are depicted in the later section). One factor that might argue against a date in the 1270s is the mention in Chapter 3 of the salt monopoly being in the hands of King Henry--most likely Henry II, just possibly Henry III--but this, too, could have been copied from an earlier model. In this copy, these lines have been inked out, presumably at a point when the salt monopoly was owned by someone else, most likely after 1294.

The swearing pages are painted on facing pages on a separate bifolio, and the gold edges to the drapery and the elaborate architectural setting with inward curving roof over the Virgin and Child, together with the gold backgrounds, suggest that they were once splendid. In the iconographical treatment the gesture of God the Father, blessing, holding up a TO globe and supporting the arms of Christ's cross all at the same time is worthy of note, and the absence of the Dove would be noteworthy if indeed it is absent and not merely rubbed out. On the Virgin's side there is an interesting parallel in the shapes of the floral motifs flanking the Virgin and Child and the similar motifs common in Tables of Affinity--which could be read as underlining the legal rôle of the Virgin and Child, here presented as the legal recipients of the act of swearing. In their present state it is hard to be sure whether or not the swearing pages are contemporary with the rest of the medieval part of the manuscript. The rest of the illumination consists of foliate initials, historiated initials, and small miniatures in rectangular frames the width of the text column to its inner ruling, with blue or pink diaper backgrounds, bounded with fillets of gold or silver/tin. The foliate accompaniments have bud-like leaves outlined with white dots (the latter possibly due to the hand of 'D.B.'), and dragon terminals and other border motifs. The colours are light green, pink, mid blue, white dots on leaf motifs, gold fillet frames, and plain or diapered pink and blue backgrounds. There are very few stylistic cognates but the foliate decoration is not without echos of the Evangeliary in Carcassonne (Carcassonne, Archives Dépärtementales de l'Aude, G 288), and although the figures in the latter are much larger in scale there are also similarities in the use of a palette of pastel shades—light blue, pink, and light green, with much use of white, and an absence of mauve.

A second hand is found from ff. 81-93v, corresponding to a change of scale (if not of scribe) in the script. The second artist was responsible for the champies, foliate initials and historiated initials in this final section. The figure drawing, however, is by the same artist throughout, despite his use of both brown and black ink for the facial features of the figures, suggesting that the change occurred as the book was in the making. The second artist also added the champies on ff. 5v and 6, corresponding in the Table of Contents to the chapters falling between ff. 81 and 93v in the text, also corresponding to the change of scale, if not of scribal hand, in the script.

The *Livre d'Agenais* made between 1283 and 1286 in Oxford (Oxford, Bodleian Library, Bodley 917), is markedly different, and closer to the *Breviary of Saintes,* perhaps of c. 1280-90 (Paris, Bibliothèque nationale de France, latin 16309) than to the *Costumas* of Agen itself, again suggesting that the *Costumas* is earlier. The use of a similar light palette is found in the early fourteenth century however, in the Franciscan devotional miscellany in Latin, French, and Occitan, for a Franciscan nun of Périgueux (London, British Library, Egerton 945).

The subjects form an unusual sequence of illustrations of the actual customs of the city, closely dependant on the words of the text. The adultery and perjury scenes here fulfill a particular rôle of displaying the consequences of crime, both emphasizing the parading of the guilty parties for public view (ff. 42v, 44v). The pierced tongue of

the false witness is especially noteworthy, as Bruna has observed. These scenes are particularly close in thematic emphasis if not in style to the astonishing series of punishments depicted in the margins of the Customary of Toulouse of 1296 noted above. The Customaries of Montauban, Cahors and Limoges lack illustrations to the text other than the swearing pages and the Gospel pericopes (in Montauban only). The Cahors swearing pages may have been reused from another manuscript, a practice also found in the *Livre juratoire* of the Bastide de Cologne (Gers). Otherwise the copies of the Digest of Justinian, although not specific to a particular place, provide the closest iconographic analogies to Agen 42 (for instance Krakow, Biblioteca Jagellonski 374, probably from Toulouse, and Berlin, Deutsche Staatsbibliothek, Hamilton 365 and Avignon, Bibliothèque Municipale, 749, both probably made in Avignon).

PROVENANCE: Made for and used by the consuls of Agen and in their possession up to the Revolution; Baret de Lavedan, conseiller à la Cour des Aides de Bordeaux, 1793, from his father, according to Abbé J. Labrunie, *Abrégé chronologique des Antiquités d'Agen,* Agen, 1892, 57-58; in Agen in 1825 when copied by M. Debeaux; in the possession of M. Debeaux, given by him to his son, who gave it to the city of Agen at his death in 1910 (Lauzun, 1910, 9-10).

EXHIBITED: *Trésors de l'enluminure en Languedoc*, ed. M. Durliat, Toulouse, 1963, 10-12, no. 12

WEB:A digital version of the complete manuscript can be viewed at the following website (October, 2008):

http://www.cg47.fr/archives/coups-de-coeur/Tresors/tresors-archives.htm

N. B. Old Occitan words appear in *italics*, English words in Roman. Noun forms with a flexional -s have been been indexed together under the form without -s. Imparisyllabic forms have been indexed together under the nominative, e.g. *vendeire*. Since the English forms appear on odd-numbered (right-hand) pages, reference to English forms will be to odd-numbered pages. However, since some Old Occitan forms appear on odd-numbered pages in square brackets, these forms have been referenced as well. Word-counts based on this index are therefore likely to be inaccurate. There are few convergences, e.g. *costs*, which is an Old Occitan word p. 84 and an English one pp. 33, 71, and 85. References to consecutive pages have been abbreviated (e.g. 66-68), but readers are alerted to the fact that since Old Occitan words appear generally on even pages, references in the index to a series of even numbers (e.g. 22, 24, 26) actually show occurrences of a word on consecutive pages of text. Only words in the Old occitan text, and the English translation, have been indexed.

www.ingramcontent.com/pod-product-compliance
Ingram Content Group UK Ltd.
Pitfield, Milton Keynes, MK11 3LW, UK
UKHW030101280625
460187UK00006B/197

9 782503 519203